Parenting
With Love
Making A Difference In A Day

Parenting With Love

Making A Difference In A Day

Glenn I. Latham

P & T ink
Logan, Utah

For my wife, Louise,
who parents with so much love

Library of Congress Catalog Card Number 99-71852
ISBN 1-57008-661-3

Fourth Printing, 2005

Printed in the United States of America

Contents

. . . .

Acknowledgments

I want to acknowledge in a special way my appreciation to Dr. Sidney Bijou, Dr. Carl Cheney, Dr. Joseph Cautela, and Dr. Waris Ishaq, for their excellent reviews of this and related work. Their suggestions contributed markedly to the technical accuracy of the manuscript.

I also acknowledge Jana Roberts for the long and tedious hours she spent typing and retyping the manuscript, and Cindy Budge for her creative help in preparing figures and tables.

Introduction

After my thirty years of working with families in trouble, I find the lament of parents is still the same: "I was never taught how to raise kids." It's pretty tough to become skillful at something about which one knows nothing!

In this book I address several specific parenting skills that are anchored in the science of human behavior. First, I present four basic principles of human behavior that are particularly relevant to parenting. Second, I describe four positive things parents absolutely need to do when their children behave well. Next, I discuss four noncoercive, instructive things parents need to do when their children misbehave. (It *is* possible to be pleasant even when kids aren't.) I conclude by alerting you to eight traps you must avoid. Getting caught in any one of them can substantially neutralize a parent's effectiveness.

At the outset, let me make three things clear. First, I have attempted to anchor the contents of this book in solid science. This science provides one of our best hopes for responsibly treating humankind's most compelling problems. Though I use anecdotes and illustrations from time to time, they are not used to prove a point; rather, they are used to drive a point home.

Second, given the vastness of the topic being addressed (i.e., parenting) it is not possible in one book to cover the width, breadth, and depth of it. Soon after he had published

. . . .

his monumental theory of relativity, Albert Einstein was asked by a reporter to give a layman's definition of relativity. Einstein replied: "When a man sits with a pretty girl for an hour, it seems like a minute. But let him sit on a hot stove for a minute—and it's longer than an hour. That's relativity." The reporter responded, "I would like something a little more technical than that." Einstein answered, "Ah, now that will take more time."

Though I address here a number of foundation issues and make some very specific, useful suggestions, there are many other sources to which a serious student of parenting could turn to deal with virtually any parenting problem; hence a list of suggested readings and other helps is found at the end of this book.

I refer to the contents of this book as "foundation issues." I have chosen that term carefully because I fully believe that no matter how much more detailed or complex or in-depth one might become in fashioning a healthy family environment, it would be built upon the foundation issues discussed in this book.

Third, it must be understood that there is no such thing as a "sure-fire" approach to parenting. There is no strategy, no matter how well founded and solidly anchored in science it might be, that will be absolutely effective with absolutely all children in absolutely any setting. Treating human behavior, like treating the human body, relies on "probable" effectiveness. We have all had the experience of going to a doctor and, upon having a medication prescribed, heard the doctor say, "Try this." Why didn't the doctor say, "This is absolutely certain to fix you up"? The answer is obvious: There was at least some chance, some possibility—however slight—that it wouldn't work for a particular individual. Nevertheless, in deciding upon the treatment a competent doctor would have done everything in his/her power to increase, to the highest level possible, the probability that the treatment would work. In some instances, those probabilities are much higher than in other instances.

And so it is with human behavior. Though in all instances we can't predict with absolute certainty the results of what we do, we do know that under certain conditions the probabilities of our "treatment" producing the desired effects are greater than in other instances. Our job, therefore, is to create an environment in which the probabilities for success are remarkably increased.

As with the practice of medicine, that is much easier done in some instances than in others. For example, the chances of eliminating the inconsolable crying of a healthy baby is much higher than is the probability of eliminating the anti-social behavior of a violent teenager who is under the influence of fellow gang members. Still, in either instance, the probabilities of being successful in moving behavior in the right direction are increased dramatically with the skillful application of what the science of human behavior has taught us.

To begin, then, the four principles of human behavior that follow are of great importance.

Chapter One

· · · · · · · · · · · · · · · · · ·

Four Basic Principles of Human Behavior

Though there are many principles of human behavior, only four are discussed here. It is my experience, after having spent a professional lifetime working with parents, that these four principles are particularly important and applicable in making home a safe and loving place.

Behavioral Principle No. 1: Behavior Is Largely a Product of Its Immediate Environment

Simply put, fix the environment and you will fix the behavior. The first lesson to be learned by parents is the importance of creating an environment in the home that will encourage and reinforce appropriate behavior.

Most home environments are reactive; that is, children behave in age-typical ways—including sibling rivalry, name calling, shouting, and even fighting—and parents react to those behaviors in kind. They shout back and they hit back and they name call, and do almost exactly what the children do. Recently, a mother was in my office complaining about the fighting between her eleven- and nine-year-old sons. She said, "Yesterday my eleven-year-old

· · · · · · ·

1

knocked his nine-year-old brother to the floor, and while his brother was on the floor crying, he kicked him!" I asked the mother what she did about it. She answered, "Well, I kicked *him!*" (meaning she kicked the eleven-year-old).

Before parents can hope to create a safe and loving home, they must learn to *proact,* not react. They must learn to create a proactive environment in the home, which I define as a positive, reinforcing, facilitating environment that is managed by stable parents. How to do this is discussed in some detail throughout this book. But I must emphasize that effective parenting is the key, effective in the sense that parents create a functional environment where: (1) *appropriate behavior is modeled;* (2) *expectations are clear and reasonable;* (3) *supervision is consistent;* (4) *behavior is monitored,* and (5) *discipline* (I prefer the term *management*) *is noncoercive.* In the vast majority of instances, we *must* quit asking the question, "What's wrong with that kid?" and instead ask, "What's wrong with that kid's environment?"

As emphasized in an article entitled "Seeking the Criminal Element," "[No] biological abnormality has been shown to *cause* violent aggression—nor is that likely except in cases of extreme . . . disorder" (Gibbs, 1997, p. 106). Such behavior is far more likely to be a matter of the "sins of the parent . . . visited on the child"; "sins" in the form of drug and alcohol abuse, coercion, beatings, crimes—and the list goes on. A list that contains *absolutely* no surprises.

In the more general sense, however, creating a proactive environment in the home can be greatly enhanced, as suggested by Cautela (1993), by "raising the general level of positive reinforcement" in the home. I have found that when the general level of positive reinforcement (GLPR) in the home is low or inappropriate, annoying behavior is high, and on the other hand, when the general level of positive reinforcement is high the incidence of inappropriate, annoying behavior is low, as illustrated in Figure 1.

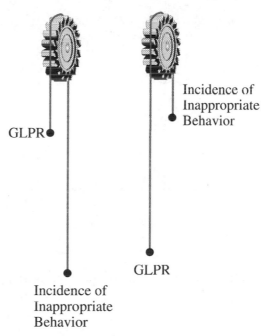

Figure 1: The relationship between the general level of positive reinforcement (GLPR) and the incidence of inappropriate behavior.

Raising the GLPR in the home can be accomplished, to a great extent, through smiling and laughter, appropriate touch, "safe" talk, and attentive listening. As illustrated in Figure 2, the frequency and duration of these kinds of interactions between parents and their children tend to decrease dramatically with age when, in fact, each of these classes of interactions should remain high in frequency and duration, regardless of age.

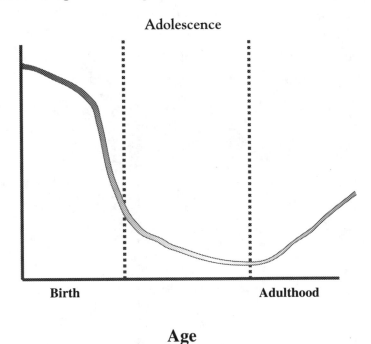

Figure 2: The decline in parent-child physical and verbal contact with age.

Smiling and Laughter

I find that as I work with families where the general level of positive reinforcement is low, people aren't smiling and laughing. Their demeanor is grim, sullen, and often stern. Their countenance has fallen, and when this is the case parents *and* children behave badly. Hitting and shouting are virtually always accompanied by stern facial expressions and an angry demeanor. I read a newspaper article recently that reported on a father's abuse of his child: "He was angry and impatient at his daughter's bed wetting." (I address this matter in more detail when I discuss Trap No. 8.)

In our present context laughter, of course, is laughter *with* not laughter *at*. It is humor that is done at no one's expense, that is wholesome and in good taste. Its therapeutic value has been well documented (Cousins, 1979). When my six children were at home, I never allowed a day go by without sharing a humorous anecdote or introducing humor in some tasteful way. It is the leaven in the loaf of parenting: it keeps things light. Tell lots of "good" jokes, and challenge your children with thought-provoking riddles, such as, "How many pairs of animals did Moses take on the ark?"

Appropriate Touch

A long history of research and clinical work documents the value of appropriate touch. The skin is the largest organ of the body, having an adult weight of about 16 pounds and an area of about 20 square feet (Rae, 1991). It contains more nerve endings than all other organs of the body combined, and it loves to be appropriately touched. Good advice in this regard is given by the U.S. Surgeon General: "Hugging is non-fattening, naturally sweet, and contains no artificial ingredients. It is wholesome and pure and, most important, fully returnable" (Staff, 1989, p. 6).

Its healing power and generally beneficial effects on health have been repeatedly documented through medical research. A study by the University of Miami Touch Research Institute found that premature babies who were massaged for fifteen minutes three times a day "were discharged from the hospital six days sooner, on average, at a current savings of $15,000 each." With 424,000 premature births in America each year, this simple therapy has the potential of generating an annual savings of *six billion* dollars!

Furthermore, premature babies who received this treatment were more alert, active, and responsive. They had fewer episodes of apnea (a risk factor for SIDS), and gained weight 45 percent faster (Colt, 1996, pp. 86–90).

Appropriate touch comes in many forms: a hug, a pat on the back, a gentle stroking of the arm, even an elbow in the ribs of an adolescent boy by his playful and affectionate father. In the raising of my children, I found no better means of communicating my love and affection for them— all the way into adulthood—than through appropriate physical touching. One of my daughters had a sign hanging on her bedroom wall that read: "Four hugs per day for survival, eight hugs for maintenance, and twelve hugs for growth."

Parents must be certain they don't allow the annoying and even distressing behaviors of their children to keep them from making appropriate physical contact. How they look and how they smell should not be deterrents. Parents often complain to me that their children don't like to be hugged, or complain at being hugged. In some instances, though rare, that might be so. Nevertheless, there are many non-hugging ways of making appropriate physical contact, including a pat on the back, a gentle stroking of the fingers across the shoulders, a squeeze of the fingers, and so on.

Safe Talk

How parents talk to their children has a huge effect on the general level of reinforcement in the home and, if used right, is a powerful tool for nurturing our children's healthy growth and development. Such interactions include shooting the breeze, verbal praise, expressions of affection, and the acknowledgment of compliant, appropriate behavior, to name a few. Unfortunately, as noted by Dr. Murray Sidman in his marvelous book *Coercion and Its Fallout* (1989), "It is not unusual to find parents who rarely speak to their children except to scold, correct, or criticize" (p. 23).

Let me give a caution. When parents shoot the breeze with their children it must be a safe interaction. This means that during the conversation there is no risk of its deteriorating into an excuse to criticize a child or to deliver some profound moral lesson that is sure to turn him off. Too often parents distort and ruin an otherwise pleasant conversation about the happenings of the day by using it as an opportunity to get some profound point across about what the child should be doing better or shouldn't be doing at all. Once children learn that there is risk of this sort, they will simply quit talking to their parents. It becomes a coercive experience, and, as noted by Sidman (1989), coercion encourages people to avoid, escape, or countercoerce (meaning to get even). Children will simply avoid talking with their parents if the probability is high that a talk will lead to an unpleasant message about one's inadequacies. Consider the following examples and non-examples of how to and how not to just shoot the breeze with children (Scenarios 1 and 2).

Scenario No. 1: Defending a Friend

Safe

Daughter:	I really feel bad for Helen. She's pregnant and her boyfriend doesn't want to have anything to do with her anymore.
Mother:	She must really feel terrible. I'm certainly proud of you, Honey, for being so concerned.
Daughter:	I don't know, Mom. It's so complex. But I am going to keep being her friend.
Mother:	Good for you. A true friend is worth more than gold. Certainly that's so in situations like this. You're a good friend, Honey. I love you.
Daughter:	I love you, Mom. It so great talking to you—even about difficult things like this. You really understand.

Unsafe

Daughter:	I really feel bad for Helen. She's pregnant and her boyfriend doesn't want to have anything to do with her anymore.
Mother:	Well, it was bound to happen. Just a matter of time. Play with fire and you get burned. I'm not the least bit surprised, nor do I feel sorry for her. She knew what she was getting into when she got mixed up with that loser. Just don't get involved. Stay clear of her. It's her problem. Let her solve it.
Daughter:	Mom! How can you say that? Helen's a neat girl. She just made a mistake. No one is per-

Mother: fect! Not you or me. Don't be so hard on her.

Mother: Neat girls don't go to bed with dumb guys. You bet she made a mistake, and she'll pay for it the rest of her life. As for you, young lady, don't you dare do a stupid thing like that.

Daughter: I can't believe you, Mother! (as she leaves in a huff).

Scenario No. 2: Defending Oneself

Safe

Dad.   That was quite a ball game last night. Your school really pulled it out of the fire in those last few minutes.

Son: Yeah. Squeaky, our point guard, was really hot.

Dad: Indeed he was. And besides his ball-handling skills, I understand he's a fine young man.

Son: He really is. He's in a couple of my classes and he's super friendly.

Dad: The next time you see him, tell him what a great job I thought he did in that game.

Son: I'll do that. He'll be happy to hear it.

Dad: Let me know when the next ball game is. Maybe we can go together.

Son: I'll do it, Dad. Sounds fun.

Dad: I'll look forward to that.

Son: Me, too. I gotta run, Dad. See ya.

Dad: So long, Son. Have a good time. Take care. Love you.

Son: Love you, too, Dad. See ya.

Unsafe

Dad: That was quite a ball game last night. Your school really pulled it out of the fire in those last few minutes.

Son: Yeah, Squeaky, our point guard, was really hot.

Dad: Indeed he was. And besides his ball-handling skills, I understand he's an excellent student who hits the books like crazy every night. What kind of GPA does he have to maintain to stay on the team?

Son: He is a good student. I have some classes with him and he does well. He has to keep at least a C+ average to be on the team.

Dad: I'm amazed he does so well with all of his athletic responsibilities. By the way, what's your GPA this year?

Son: I don't know for sure. Somewhere between a C and a C+.

Dad: Now, Son, you can surely do better than that. Surely you have more time to study than Squeaky does. I mean, with the amount of time you have, you should have a solid B average—or better!

Son: I'm doing all right in school. I'm passing. What's the big deal?

Dad: Just passing! I know you can do better than that. If a kid on the basketball team can do it, you can. You're just as smart as Squeaky.

Son: Hey, what's this all about? What has Squeaky got to do with me? He lives his life and I live mine, and that's just how I want it!

Dad: I'll tell you what it's about. It's about your life. Without decent grades it's the end of school for you. Just look at Squeaky. I'll bet he not only gets accepted into college, but he'll get an athletic scholarship as well. He's got his head on straight. You could use a little of that head-on-straight stuff, young man!

Son: Forget it. I'm outta here. I don't need this garbage.

Recent research in the field of verbal behavior has given special meaning and importance to "safe" talk. Drs. Betty Hart and Todd Risley (1995) in their marvelous study published under the title *Meaningful Differences in the Everyday Experience of Young American Children* report that in what I call low-risk families, by age four years old, children heard approximately 45 million words, of which six times more were positive than negative. Furthermore, the language used by parents was "rich" and descriptive, with positive things being said just over thirty times per hour. Under such conditions, it is hard to imagine anything but a safe and loving place.

Another study, reported in the *Behavior Analysis Digest* (Wyatt, Summer 1997) suggested that "spoken language has an astonishing impact on an infant's brain development. In fact, some researchers say the number of words an infant hears each day is the single most important predictor of later intelligence, school success, and social competence. There is one catch—the words have to come from an attentive, engaged human being. As far as anyone has been able to determine, radio and television do not work" (pp. 1, 6). In this regard, I encourage parents of infants to carry those children so they can look them in the face, whether that be carrying the baby on the hip, or in a baby carrier strapped to the parent's body. This provides additional opportunities to speak to a child, smile, and even tenderly touch, face-to-face. Which brings me to the next important point in making home a safe and loving place: attentive listening.

Attentive Listening

Parents need to listen attentively to their children with interest and understanding. It is behavior that says "I'm with you": eye-to-eye contact, expressive facial gestures, brief verbal acknowledgments, leaning forward, and other posturings that signal attentiveness. It means turning off the television, putting down the newspaper or book, and eliminating other distractors that get in the way of being attentive. As a distraught teenager once told me: "My parents never look me in the eye when we talk. It's always through a newspaper, or with an occasional glance away from the TV; or when I know very well they are preoccupied by something else, and whatever I have to say is really of no importance." We are not talking rocket science here, folks. What I'm advising is easy to do, and wonderfully effective.

Remember, behavior is largely a product of its immediate environment; therefore, the responsibility of parents is to create a stable, proactive environment in the home; that is, a positive, supportive, facilitating environment. Appropriately shape the environment and the environment will shape the behavior. Attentive listening is a powerful tool in the shaping of such an environment.

Behavioral Principle No. 2:
Behavior Is Shaped by Consequences

It is what follows behavior that determines whether that behavior will be repeated (Bijou, 1993, pp. 63–68). As noted by Dr. Aubrey Daniels in his splendid book *Bringing Out the Best in People* (1994), "People do what they do because of what happens to them when they do it" (p. 25). In a home and family setting this takes on a special meaning, given the frequency and quality of interactions between parents and their children.

Of all the consequences that reinforce the behavior of children, I have found nothing to be more powerful than parental attention. Over the years, as I have worked with families, I have been interested to note that, on average, more than 95 percent of all appropriate child behavior never receives any parental attention whatsoever. It is simply ignored, very much in harmony with that unfortunate, generations-old caution to "leave well enough alone." On the other hand, parents are five to six times more likely to pay attention to their children when the children are behaving inappropriately.

Now, the question arises: If behavior is shaped by consequences, if parental attention to behavior is a powerful consequence, and if the behaviors that receive parental attention are annoying, inappropriate behaviors, which behaviors are being reinforced? The answer is obvious: annoying, inappropriate behaviors. For the most part, ironically, the very behaviors that annoy and concern parents most are the very behaviors parents are encouraging; hence, those are the behaviors that are most likely to reoccur predictably. We have spotted the enemy, and it is us! (Thanks, Pogo.)

Children can get so starved for parental attention that there are almost no lengths to which they will not go to get it. The young parents of two small children told me they were concerned that they were giving inordinate amounts of attention to their children when they behaved in an annoying or inappropriate way, and that virtually all of that attention was unpleasant and aversive. "We were raised this way, and promised ourselves we would not treat our children the way we had been treated. But here we are doing the very same things to our children that we hated having done to us when we were children. We know that our children annoy us to get our attention, which is what we did when we were children. We soon learned that the only way to get our parents' attention was to do something bad, and even though the attention we got was usually unpleasant, even painful, it was better than no attention at all." (As will be discussed later, a critical foundation skill in parenting is being able to distinguish consequential from inconsequential behavior, and to respond appropriately to each.)

As I have visited with young people around the globe, I have asked many of them the question, "Why do you *do* what your parents tell you to do?" Virtually without exception, their answers are the same: "I do it because if I don't, I'm in trouble." It is a tragedy that, for the most part, children do what they are told to do to escape the unpleasant consequences of not complying rather than to enjoy the positive consequences of behaving well. Which brings us to Behavioral Principle No. 3.

Behavioral Principle No. 3: Behavior Is Ultimately Shaped Better by Positive Than by Negative Consequences

In the *International Encyclopedia of Education* (Bijou, 1988), Dr. Sidney Bijou has given us the Golden Rule of effective parenting: "Research has shown that the most effective way to reduce problem behavior in children is to strengthen desirable behavior through positive reinforcement rather than trying to weaken undesirable behavior using aversive or negative processes."

Despite this well-documented behavioral fact, the overwhelming inclination of parents is to try to control their children's behavior by using aversive, negative, and/or coercive processes. In other words, parents try to *make* their children behave by using threats, physical force, verbal outbursts of anger and so on (discussed in detail in Strategy No. 4: Parent Traps). Recalling again Dr. Murray Sidman's work (1989), coercive efforts to control behavior encourage people to want to escape or avoid the coercer, and when able to do so, countercoerce (meaning, get even).

This was dramatically illustrated for me while waiting to catch a plane. Seated across from me in the passenger lounge was a young family composed of a mother, a father, and a little boy—who I estimated to be about five years old. The boy was sitting between his parents and was engaging in a lot of the age-typical behaviors of a little boy about to get into a huge airplane and fly off into the sky. He was giddy and a bit rambunctious, and obviously very excited to get on board.

The father became more and more annoyed at the boy's behavior. Abruptly, he looked angrily at the boy and, raising his hand in a menacing gesture, said harshly, "Sit down and be quiet or I'm going to smack you one!" The little boy immediately sat still. Very still, in fact. He looked up sadly into his father's face. After about a minute he quietly slipped off his seat and took the empty seat on the other side of his mother, getting as far away from his father as he could, under the circumstances. As he settled in, he snuggled up closely to his mother, putting both arms around her arm and pulling himself close to her for safety and security. That little boy, in the face of coercion, quietly avoided and escaped his father. Imagine what will happen between this boy and his father ten or twelve years from now when the boy is not only able to escape and avoid but is also able to countercoerce!

We see countercoercion being acted out by adolescent children all of the time in the form of skipping school, staying out late at night, eagerly violating home rules, stealing money from parents and other family members, and the list goes on and on.

Negative, aversive, coercive methods of managing behavior are insidious for at least two reasons. First, they create the appearance of being effective. That is, like the little boy in the air terminal who fell silent beneath the rage of his father, children will often immediately comply, giving the parent reason to believe that what was done worked: the kid shaped up immediately. What the parent doesn't realize is that the behavior that was attacked coercively continues to repeat itself time after time after time. Coercion has no positive, lasting effect on improving behavior. The child isn't learning a better way of behaving; hence he continues to behave in the same maladaptive way, only to be responded to by the parent in an equally maladaptive way. Remember this: *Short-term compliance achieved using coercive means ultimately leads to long-term losses.* Please! Never forget that!

The second reason why negative, aversive, coercive measures are insidious is that they have acquired pseudo-validity, meaning a false sense of worth, by having been woven into the fabric of child rearing for generations—even millennia. It goes like this: "That's how my grandfather raised my dad, and it's how my dad raised me. We turned out okay, so that's the way I'm going to raise my kids." It is that very same vacuous mentality that has produced the tyrants of our age: Joseph Stalin, Adolf Hitler, Saddam Hussein. . . . In a recent newspaper article chronicling the rise of Mao Tse-tung as "An Inept Ruler and the Twentieth Century's Greatest Revolutionary," the author noted that "a cruel father and a difficult earlier teacher bred in him the spirit of rebellion that led naturally to revolution" (Roderick, 1994). A perfect description of the long-term effects of coercion leading to countercoercion. Violence breeds violence. Patience and kindness breed patience and kindness.

My caution to parents everywhere is this: *Do and say to your children only what you want done and said to your grandchildren.* Coercion produces, at best, only short-term compliance, and at worst long-term losses. My work with families reveals that coercion enters the parent-child relationship when the child is beginning to acquire functional language—usually around fourteen months. It is about this age when children learn that there is power in the word *no*.

17

Typically when a child says no to a parental directive, the parent will respond harshly, coercively with a swat on the bottom, or an angry "Don't you say no to me! Now you do what I tell you to do."

Getting the desired response (that is, immediate compliance) convinces the parent that coercion is how to get results. Over time, the coercive approach to forced obedience builds and builds. As coercion accumulates, it puts distance between the child and the parent(s) as the child escapes and avoids an unsafe relationship. As the child moves into adolescence, this wedge is driven deeper and deeper until at about 14½ the child will take no more, as illustrated in Figure 3. He or she will tell the parent, "I don't want to and you can't make me," as things go from

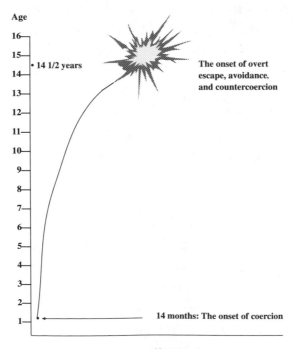

Figure 3: The negative effects of coercion over time.

· · · · · · ·

bad to worse: long-term losses produced by years of ill-gotten short-term compliance.

Behavioral Principle No. 4: Past Behavior Is the Best Predictor of Future Behavior

Unless something is done to interrupt or redirect the course of a behavior, the chances are great that the behavior will continue as it has in the past. True, children do outgrow some behaviors. Also, some behaviors will improve as the individual's circumstances change. Remember, behavior is largely a product of its immediate environment, so as one's environment changes, so will that person's behavior. One study reported "that of 209 hyper aggressive preschoolers predicted to develop antisocial behavior, 177 did not" (Gibbs, 1997, p. 107). The only conclusion one can draw is that something happened in the lives of those 177 children that made behaving nonaggressively more reinforcing than behaving aggressively; that is, the course of their behavior was somehow redirected by the changing of events in their environment: new friends, moving to a different neighborhood, being shown a special interest by a teacher or relative, and so on.

The point of all this is a simple one: if things are going to get better, something has to change for the better. My message is that making that change is the responsibility of the parents. If achieving healthy change is left to chance, the risk of the unhealthy way winning out is too great. But as with the 177 in the earlier cited study, it can happen for the better if what happens is better. It doesn't take a neurosurgeon to figure that one out.

Often parents simply can't believe things can change. They have bought into the past with such conviction that they cannot imagine it otherwise. I recall the parents of a seventeen-year-old son who, though they came to me for help, were sure it was "too late." Still, they felt compelled to "give it one last shot."

After I had gotten a firm commitment out of the parents that they would go forward with hope, get their chins up off their chests, smile, ease up, and do what I told them to do, we got to work. We role-played how to state expectations, how to select and apply consequences, how to step aside and let consequences deliver the message, and how to replace coercive parenting with noncoercive parenting. They went on their way with new tools and fresh hope.

A few days before this writing, after I had delivered a talk to a large gathering of parents, a couple approached me. I recognized them as the parents of the seventeen-year-old boy for whom it was "too late." This is what they told me: "We thought you'd like to know. He's off drugs, quit smoking and drinking, and is in school. He'll graduate by the end of the year. He's even saving money for a mission. We would never have believed it could happen."

Now, don't assume that it always turns out this way. But it frequently does. In fact, in time, the vast, vast majority—over 90 percent—eventually *do* get their lives together and become productive, law-abiding citizens. But something has to change, otherwise past behavior *will* be future behavior.

The next chapter describes specific things parents should do when their children behave well, since, as noted by Bijou (1988), "Research has shown that the most effective way to strengthen desirable behavior in children is through the use of positive reinforcement" (p. 448).

Chapter Two

. . . .

What to Do When Children Behave Well

In my three decades working with parents, a parent has yet to come to me and ask the most important question of all: "What do I do when my child behaves well?" If the day ever comes when parents look first for opportunities to positively acknowledge their children's appropriate behavior, rather than waiting to react negatively and coercively when they misbehave, a whole new era will have dawned for parents as child rearers. When that day comes, the business of parenting and the business of growing up will become much easier and much more pleasant for parents and children.

In this chapter I discuss four things parents should do when their children behave well. To be effective, each of these must be an integral part of a whole. Parents must become skillful with each of these strategies and be able to use them in a timely, consistent manner. Any one of these, used alone, is simply not adequate.

Strategy No. 1: Verbally Acknowledge Appropriate Behavior in a Positive Way

I was invited to give a talk to a large group of high

. . . .

school students about the importance of positive human interactions. When I concluded, the teacher did something that left a lasting impression on me. She asked the students to indicate, by a show of hands, how many of them were regularly criticized by their parents for the things they did wrong. Every hand shot into the air. The teacher then asked, by a show of hands, how many were regularly praised by their parents for the things they did right. Not one single hand went up.

For starters, I suggest that parents keep a written record of the quality of the interactions between them and their children, using a simple tally form shown in Figure 4. I ask parents to describe the interaction and then indicate whether it was a positive interaction or a negative interaction, with the goal being that they should make a conscious effort to have no more than one negative interaction for every eight positive interactions. This is highly consistent with the findings of Drs. Betty Hart and Todd Risley that I shared earlier. As you might recall, they found that in "low-risk" families, parents were six times more likely to say positive rather than negative things to their children.

Taking data on yourself can be a real pain. I know that. I'm taking data on my behavior all the time, and I've been doing it for thirty years. But it's worth the effort. Someone once noted that "Behavior that is measured is behavior that is improved." I believe that with all my heart. At the time of this writing, I am taking data on my behavior behind the wheel of my car, and I'm doing a *lot* better. Even my wife has commented on how much more patient I am. Furthermore, she has commented on how much more patient I am in other settings. That's one of the wonderful things about working on your behavior. Good behavior generalizes.

Description of the Interaction	+	−

Figure 4: Assessing the quality of parent-child interacting

As I behave better in one setting (like while I'm driving), before long I'm behaving better in other settings (like while shopping with my wife—which I've hated doing with every fiber of my being! But I'm better now. I only hate it now with half the fibers of my being!)

Parents are five to six times more likely to attend to their children when they behave inappropriately than when they behave appropriately. What I am suggesting is a strategy that will reverse that and will head parents in the right direction. The hope, of course, is that negative interactions will cease altogether. As parents and grandparents, my wife and I virtually never have negative interactions with our children or grandchildren. To do so would be absurd. It is so inefficient and counterproductive.

Evidence of the value of a positive rather than a negative approach to problem solving was nicely illustrated by a student of mine (Reed, 1994) who was concerned about the "incessant whining" of his six-year-old daughter. He took data for one week on the quality of his interactions with his daughter, including the frequency of her whining behavior. He took the data between 4:00 and 8:00 P.M. each day, since these were the times when he was most likely to be home with her. As described below, on average she whined thirteen times each day, during which time he averaged ten negative interactions and only three positive interactions. The ratio of negative to positive interactions was a little greater than three to one. Following is a description of Reed's *positive* approach to problem solving, and a report on the results. Figure 5 graphically portrays the effect of treatment.

1. *Problem Behavior*: My six-year-old daughter whined too often about too many things, and I was too negative/coercive when she did.

2. *Baseline Data:* I took data for one week, between 4:00
   P.M. and 8:00 P.M. each day. Here are the average
   number of times the critical behaviors occurred:
   Average number of times my daughter whined: 13
   Average number of times I was negative/coercive: 10
   Average number of times I was positive: 3

Average Weekly Responses

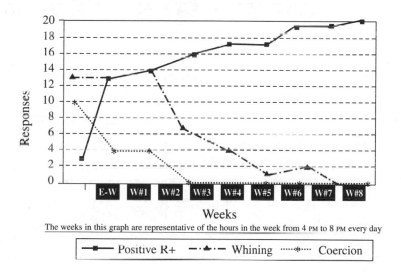

The weeks in this graph are representative of the hours in the week from 4 PM to 8 PM every day

— ■ — Positive R+   — ▲ — Whining   ⋯ ✳ ⋯ Coercion

Figure 5. The effects of treatment on the elimination of whining behavior.

3. *Problem-Solving Procedure:*
   - *Target Behavior*: To eliminate my daughter's whining,
     and to eliminate my being negative/coercive.
   - *Intervention*: Put whining behavior on extinction, and
     selectively reinforce non-whining behavior.
4. *Results*: After seven weeks, the whining behavior
   was completely gone, and by the eighth week, I was

averaging twenty positive interactions per day and no negative/coercive interactions. Also, my daughter's appropriate behavior generalized to several other desirable behaviors, without any formal intervention, including:

- Getting out of bed in the morning without being told.
- Making her bed daily.
- Getting ready for the day without the usual help from Mom and Dad by (a) dressing herself, (b) combing her hair, and (c) putting her stuffed animals on her bed.
- Setting the table for breakfast.
- Following her parents' model by hugging and reinforcing her brothers, sisters, and Mom and Dad.
- Being generally helpful with family/home activities.

It is interesting that in addition to improvement in the target behavior, the child began engaging in so many other appropriate behaviors without any formal intervention. This is called the generalization effect. The fruits of positive consequences.

Strategy No. 2:
Acknowledge Appropriate Behavior Intermittently, Meaning Randomly or Every Once in a While

The power of the intermittent schedule of reinforcement in shaping behavior is well documented. In fact, it's the most powerful schedule of reinforcement known. Getting a reinforcer at a moment when one least expects it has the most powerful effect on keeping behavior going. It keeps lottery systems going, it keeps golf courses in business, and it is the very core of the Nevada economy. I think you get the point.

I suggest that parents have numerous positive interactions with their children per hour, interactions that are delivered intermittently in the form of a touch, a wink, a smile, or a pleasant verbal acknowledgment of what was done that brought parental attention (which is addressed more completely below in strategies 3 and 4). It is not unreasonable for parents to aim at having twenty or more brief, intermittent positive interactions per hour with their children, particularly young children, four to five years old and below. The result will be high rates of appropriate behavior and few if any inappropriate behaviors.

To help parents remember to have a sufficient number of intermittently delivered positive interactions, I further suggest that they use a few well-placed reminders. Some of the parents I've advised put a nickel or a quarter in their shoes. Occasionally (i.e., intermittently) as they become conscious of the coin being there, they are reminded, "Have I had a positive interaction with my children?" Some parents will tilt a picture on the wall a little off level as a reminder. Others will place a knickknack or a flower or some other decorative item out of place. Some even put a loose-fitting rubber band around their wrist. When they see the item out of place, or whatever, it reminds them to have a positive interaction with their children. Without some sort of a crutch—i.e., a prosthetic (Lindsley, 1963)— to lean on, the events of the day can become so hectic that parents simply forget to have an appropriate number of positive interactions with their children, delivered in a random, intermittent manner. As discussed in strategy number 3 below, when done appropriately twenty or more brief, intermittently delivered positive reinforcers per hour is not at all unreasonable.

Strategy No. 3: Acknowledge Appropriate Behavior Casually and Briefly

As parents happen upon their children who are behaving appropriately, that is the time to deliver a positive reinforcer. As unaffected and unceremoniously as possible, a parent should acknowledge the behavior using only a few words (no more than eight to twelve), and taking only a few seconds (three to five are plenty), and then move on to other things. For example, suppose that two children are playing nicely together and "playing nicely together" is a behavior the parent wants to see more of. The parent would casually walk by the children, say, "You children are having lots of fun playing together so nicely," give them a smile and perhaps a gentle touch, then move on.

This example took fewer than a dozen words, and about three seconds to say. This being the case, if parents have twenty interactions per hour and each interaction takes only three seconds, that means the parent is spending only one minute per hour in positive interactions with their children. Surely that isn't too much to ask of any parent! Typically, parents spend much more time than that being negative to their children. Again, quoting Dr. Murray Sidman, "It is not unusual to find parents who rarely speak to their children except to scold, correct, or criticize."

It is critical that these positive interactions be casual and occur in the normal course of a parent's comings and goings through the house, or while with the child elsewhere: grocery shopping, at the park, at the homes of friends and relatives, at church, or wherever. Frequent positive interactions, delivered casually and briefly and intermittently, cumulatively can have a powerful reinforcing effect on behavior.

Strategy No. 4:
Give Variety to Verbal Praise

Descriptive Praise

As emphasized earlier, when verbal praise is used to reinforce a behavior it is important that the parent occasionally use language that describes the behavior being reinforced. Rather than simply saying "good boy" or "good girl," the parents would describe the behavior being attended to: "Thank you for coming to dinner when I called you," "Thank you for being so kind to your sister," "I like the way you're working so hard on your homework."

It is interesting but not unusual for a child to occasionally react inappropriately to such verbal praise. For example, suppose that a brother says something nice to his sister, and the parent decides to acknowledge that by saying, "Billy, I appreciate you being so kind to your sister." It isn't at all unlikely that Billy might look up at the parent and say, "I hate my sister! She's the dumbest thing I've ever known." Should this or a similarly inappropriate response follow the delivery of verbal praise, the parent should simply smile, then walk on without the slightest acknowledgment of the boy's comments. All of the attention should be left only on the positive character of the boy's interaction with his sister, as discussed in more detail below.

Verbal praise that is delivered descriptively becomes instructive, and in time children will learn what it is that gets their parents' attention. They learn that if inappropriate behavior is not attended to, it is foolish to waste time on it!

If the environment has traditionally been reactive and parents have tended to use coercive, negative, and aversive methods for managing behavior, the shift to a positive, proactive approach might prompt children to increase, temporarily, the frequency and duration of inappropriate behavior. This is called an extinction burst (Sulzer-Azaroff and Mayer, 1991, p. 409). That is, the behavior might get worse, temporarily, before it gets better. If that happens, parents should not be alarmed; rather, they should stick with the program; and within a short period of time, generally within a few days at most, the inappropriate behavior will begin to fade rapidly and appropriate behavior will rush in to fill the void, and even increase in duration, frequency, and type, as was illustrated earlier by Reed (1994).

What parents need to realize is that behavior is largely a product of its immediate environment, and once children learn that well-placed positive consequences issue from appropriate behavior, and that the environment is rich with positive reinforcers for appropriate behavior, those are the behaviors that will most likely reoccur. Remember, when the general level of positive reinforcement is high, inappropriate behavior is low. It's as simple as that. But it takes time to get a treatment effect, so be patient and stick with the program. Even the best medicine doesn't cure an illness instantaneously!

Deserved Praise

Praise should be given only when it is deserved. Heaping praise on children for everything they do well or right results in what we call "satiation," and kids tire of it. It begins to ring hollow. It gets old and soon becomes distasteful. I like ice cream, but I don't like a quart of it at every meal.

Sincere Praise

When praising a child, make sure you mean it or at least sound like you mean it. Deliver it with a smile on your face and a twinkle in your eye, even if the child gives you an expression of not caring in the least about what you're saying. Even if he rolls his eyes to the ceiling, or she says, with indifference, "Okay, Mother. Okay. I get it." Michael Resnick (1997) and his colleagues, reporting on the influences of adult interactions and expectations on teen behavior, found that even though adolescents might appear unaffected, and even turned off, by what parents say, in the long run—typically beyond adolescence—it pays off. An experience several years ago with our youngest son illustrates that nicely. As he was about to head off to a university far away for graduate studies, he said to his mother: "Mom, I'm doing exactly what I promised myself as a boy I'd never do. I'm behaving just like Dad."

Values-Rich Praise

It is a sad but well-documented matter of fact that today's youth tend to have an alarmingly weak sense of, or appreciation for, values and "common moral decencies" that, over the centuries, have "maximized human happiness and minimized suffering" (Newman, et al., 1996, p. 279). I'm talking about kindness, loyalty, goodness, tolerance, honesty, hard work, appreciation, service to others, selflessness, generosity, dependability . . . you know what I mean. An inclination toward such basic indicators of civility is growing weaker by the day. One author (Lake, 1997, p. 3) under the title "Society's Ugly New Attitude: 'You Don't Mind If I'm Rude Do You?'" observed that "civility, if not dead, is dying." We see it everywhere: a professional athlete spits in his coach's face, selfishness in traffic, littering, defacing, not flushing the toilet, butting in line, letting the door close in the face of the person following behind, failure to say please and thank you, rude and profane comments about others, cheating, and the list goes on.

For the past generation particularly, parents have been so concerned about their children's compliance that they have forgotten values, morals, and decency. Reacting to the Supreme Court decision banning prayer in school, many public school teachers were cautioned—and in many instances instructed—to avoid teaching morals and values for fear that they would be accused of mixing church and state, and hauled into court. And we are now paying dearly for it: 4000 people are murdered each year by kids without a conscience (Eftimiades, et al., 1997, p. 46). Youth violence is rampant. Children are committing more crimes—worse crimes—at an earlier age than ever before (many in their pre-teen years), and feeling little to no remorse for doing it. Valueless and moral-free behavior gone wild! An article in the *Reader's Digest* (Leo, 1998, p. 75) reported on the results of a study among college students regarding the Holocaust. It revealed that 10 to 20 percent of the students interviewed "acknowledged the fact of the Holocaust but [could not] bring themselves to say that killing millions of people is morally wrong."

We must reverse that, now! You can begin at home by simply embellishing the acknowledgment of compliant behavior with a statement of values:

- "Thanks for helping with the dishes" (compliance). "That's being a *hard worker*" (values).
- "You did a good job getting your homework done" (compliance). "Thank you for being *dependable*" (values).
- "I was impressed at how *kind* and *helpful* you were while tending the baby" (values added to values).

So long as children are only making choices between right and wrong, good and bad, do or don't, they will always be close to danger. But when their choices are elevated to the level of values, it becomes a matter of good, better, or best, in which case almost any decision will be a healthy one. Give that serious thought, Mom and Dad.

Chapter Three

. . . .

What to Do When Children Misbehave

Occasionally, even in the most proactive, positive environment, children will behave badly. Here I discuss four things parents should do when their children behave inappropriately. Again, each of these strategies is a part of a working whole. In fact, when the four preceding skills related to appropriate behavior are used in conjunction with the four skills about to be described relative to inappropriate behavior, the net effect is a system of parental behavior management that is almost certain to succeed in child rearing. A fitting analogy is found in Aesop's fable about the bundle of sticks: individually, each stick can be broken easily, but bound together into a bundle they are almost impossible to break.

How to respond to inappropriate behavior begins by determining whether the behavior is inconsequential or consequential. To state it briefly, inconsequential behaviors only annoy. Consequential behaviors can result in people being hurt, property being damaged or destroyed, and/or an environment being ruined. Strategies No. 1 and No. 2 are used with inconsequential behaviors. Strategy No. 3 is used with consequential behaviors. Strategy No. 4 is used in any setting

. . . .

The following three questions can help us determine whether the inappropriate behavior is consequential or inconsequential:

1. What is the probability of the behavior being harmful or damaging?
2. What is the probability of the behavior persisting beyond simple annoyance? For example, the child just won't "let it go." He/she hounds, begs, pleads, complains, carries on . . . you know what I mean.
3. What is the probability that though the behavior might begin as inconsequential, it will ultimately disintegrate into a consequential behavior? For example, children begin just teasing each other but before long they are fighting to hurt.

If any of these probabilities are low, treat the behavior as inconsequential, using Strategies No. 1 or No. 2. If any of these probabilities are high, use Strategy No. 3.

Strategy No. 1: Ignore Inconsequential Behavior

When dealing with inconsequential, age-typical, "junk," garden variety, weed behavior—that is, behavior that does not threaten persons or property—the single best response is to simply ignore it; just pay it no attention. As I have studied behavior in families, I have been interested to note that about 98 percent of the behaviors children engage in that annoy their parents are inconsequential behaviors that should simply be walked away from. Most sibling rivalry, most name calling, most tantrums, most out-of-sorts behaviors, though annoying, are of no consequence whatsoever and simply deserve no parental attention. When left alone, they tend to fade away without a trace, usually in less than two minutes. It's when parents make a big fuss about those things, scold children, get after them, threaten them, and so on, that these behaviors tend to persist.

I had an experience with my two-year-old grandson that beautifully illustrates the power of the extinction strategy in dealing with inconsequential behaviors. He and I were playing with his Lego toys when all of a sudden, for no apparent reason, he threw a Lego toy at me. Without appearing to be the least bit upset or affected by this, I simply stood up and walked away. To have said something like, "You shouldn't throw Lego toys at Grandpa. You could hurt Grandpa," would have been totally inappropriate and would have served no function other than to reinforce the inappropriate behavior.

I stayed away for about thirty seconds then returned to the table where he was playing, and picked up where I had left off, without saying a word. I certainly didn't say something dumb like, "Now if you'll play nicely, Grandpa will play with you." Saying something like that would simply have reinforced the very behavior I wanted to get rid of. Rather, I just sat down and started playing Lego toys as though there had been no interruption. Only a few seconds passed before my grandson threw another toy at me. Again, I just turned and walked away, repeating exactly what I had done before. (It's called multiple-trial learning.) After 30 to 40 seconds, when he was playing nicely with the toys, I returned and began playing with him again, as though nothing had interrupted our play. After a few seconds he picked up a Lego toy and pretended he was going to throw it at me. But he stopped, looked at me and smiled, put the Lego toy down, and began playing with it appropriately. It was at this point that I acknowledged his appropriate behavior by saying, "Thank you for playing so nicely with your Lego toys." That was the end of any inappropriate behavior on my grandson's part. Without one single critical or coercive reaction the inappropriate behavior was gone, and it was replaced immediately with high rates of appropriate behavior.

Strategy No. 2: Selectively Reinforce Other Appropriate Behavior

When adult attention is directed toward children who are behaving appropriately, though other children are behaving inappropriately, the probability is great that the inappropriate behavior will soon extinguish, and before long all the children will be behaving as they should. A few years ago I was invited by a school district to do some inservice training of teachers of emotionally disturbed children. For reasons unknown to me the district was experiencing an inordinate amount of behavior problems in the schools, particularly in their self-contained classes for seriously emotionally disturbed and behaviorally disordered children.

When my host and I arrived at the first classroom to be visited, we were met by sheer pandemonium. In fact, we had to quickly step aside as a boy ran out of the classroom with the teacher in hot pursuit. The classroom (as shown in Figure 6) had two outside doors, and out of the other door ran the aide chasing another boy. Across the room a third boy was standing on some bookcases, and just as we entered the classroom he leaped into the air trying to grab the light fixture hanging from the ceiling. Fortunately he missed the light fixture, though he went crashing to the floor knocking over a chair in the process. Within a matter of only a few seconds, the classroom teacher returned dragging a kicking and screaming kid behind her. She was followed shortly thereafter by the aide dragging another child into the classroom. As the classroom teacher went past us, my host, a school district official, whispered to her, "We need to talk," and they left the classroom. That left five wild kids, the aide (who by now was crying), and me. I walked over to the aide and asked her if I could be of help. Choking back the tears, she said, "Yes, please."

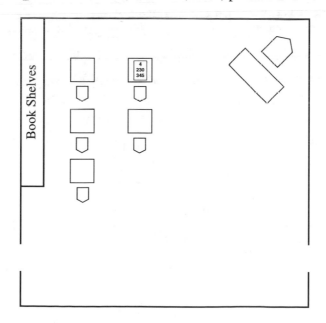

Figure 6: Classroom configuration

I quickly surveyed the situation and decided that I was simply going to put all of the inappropriate behavior on extinction, and select an appropriate behavior that was worth acknowledging. Unfortunately, none of the children were behaving in an appropriate way, so I had to look for something that approximated appropriate behavior. I was happy to find it in the form of a worksheet lying on the desk of one of the students. Without saying a word or even making eye-to-eye contact with any of the students, I walked over to the desk where the worksheet was lying and looked at it intently. In fact, I began interacting with it as though it was alive: I ran my finger across the page, moving deliberately from problem to problem. I nodded my head in approval of problems that had been answered correctly. I even vocally interacted with the paper by saying, "Yes, this problem is done correctly. That's good."

Before I began this intervention, I set my stopwatch on zero. I wanted to see how long it would take to get the students in their seats and on task using only positive methods. It has been my experience over the years that, when the situation is addressed appropriately, such results can be accomplished under positive conditions within a minute and forty-five seconds.

Within about twenty-two seconds, the boy who sat at the desk where I was standing sat down. I immediately patted him on the back, looking him squarely in the eye, and with a smile on my face, quietly said, "Thank you for taking your seat." (I avoided *any* reference to his out-of-seat behavior, such as, "You little animal, it's about time you sat down!" To have said that would have been to behave worse than the boy.)

We then began discussing his work. A few seconds later another student sat down at his desk across the aisle. I told the boy with whom I first began to work to complete a few other problems, and said I would be right back. I then moved to the boy who had just taken his seat and said: "Thank you for taking your seat. May I see your work?" He immediately took a social studies assignment out of his desk and began to explain it to me. Again, I directed my complete attention to this boy and the appropriate manner in which he was responding. Almost instantly the other three children took their seats and, in turn, I visited them all. From the time I set my stopwatch until every child was in his or her seat engaged in appropriate academic behavior, only about 1 minute and 39 seconds had elapsed, and at no point had I raised my voice above a whisper.

Though this illustration relates to a classroom experience, the same success, the same results, can be realized in homes. By a parent's selectively reinforcing the appropriate behavior of other children, while putting on extinction all inconsequential inappropriate behaviors, the inappropriate behaviors will ultimately fade away, the victim of no parental attention.

Strategy No. 3: Stop, Redirect, Then Reinforce Consequential Behavior

Occasionally, children will behave in ways that can't be ignored. These are what I call consequential behaviors, and they include verbal and physical assaults that could hurt others, be damaging to property, or might be damaging to the child himself/herself. Obviously, it would be irresponsible to just walk away from such situations.

The typical approach parents use to deal with such behavior is to call out in loud and angry tones, "Stop that, and stop it right now!" The parent might even intervene physically by jerking or spanking or hitting the child. Once the behavior has been stopped, the parent then typically delivers a tongue-lashing, punctuated with ill-chosen, inappropriate, unenforceable threats, then storms off in a huff. Though the behavior may have stopped for the moment, the child has been told only what not to do, has not learned anything about behaving appropriately; and the quality of the environment in the home has deteriorated to the point of being nothing but negative, reactive, and coercive. Rather than simply stopping inappropriate, consequential behavior, parents need to redirect the child's behavior into something appropriate that can subsequently be reinforced. I call it the stop, redirect, reinforce strategy.

For example, suppose that an older brother is hitting his younger sibling with the intent of being hurtful. Calmly, resolutely, and in complete control of his/her own emotions, the parent should move close to the assailant and, if there's no likelihood that the assailant will strike back at the parent, the parent should put his/her hand on the child's shoulder, look directly into the child's eyes for a few seconds, then say in a calm, controlled voice, "No, Son, that behavior is not acceptable in this house."

Care should be taken that nothing is said about the fighting behavior, nor that a big to-do is made about how someone might get hurt, and so on. As with the delivery of verbal praise, only a few words should be used and only a few seconds should be taken to say them. The child may argue back by saying something like, "Well, it was her fault. You're always picking on me. She gets away with everything. I hate her guts!" Even so, the parent must respond proactively, with empathy and understanding, by saying something like: "I can tell you're very upset. I can imagine how you might feel this way. Nevertheless, that behavior is not acceptable in this house." The child might complain again: "Well, what are you going to do with *her*? She started it!" Don't try to answer the question by saying something like, "What I do is my business!" In times of emotional upheaval you neither ask nor answer questions—for reasons I'll discuss in Strategy No. 4. Rather, again, using empathy and understanding, say, "I know that bothers you, but tell me how *you* should behave, even if your sister bugs you?"

When parents are confronted with angry, defensive outbursts, the absolutely best approach is to respond with empathy and understanding, while focusing on what the child is expected to do. In such an environment, the likelihood of the child arguing more than a few times in defense of his inappropriate behavior is very remote. (My data show that 97 out of 100 times, when such a strategy is employed, the child will not complain more than three times.)

Once the child's anger has subsided and the inappropriate behavior has stopped, it is time to redirect the behavior. It is at this point that the parent tells the child what he is expected to do. This could include any number of things: go outside and play, keep your hands and feet to yourself, do a chore that is waiting to be done, and so on. It might go like this:

Father: "You may remain here, Son, but I expect you to keep your hands and feet to yourself."

Son: "But it wasn't my fault! You want me to leave her alone even though she started it. That isn't fair! I'd like to beat her brains out!"

Father: "I'm sorry you're so upset, Son, but if you want to stay in this room, you'll need to keep your hands and feet to yourself."

Son: "Well, what are you going to do to her? She started it. I ought to be able to finish it."

Father: "Son, if you want to remain here, how are you going to have to behave?

Son: "You want me to keep my hands and my feet to myself. But what I want to do is punch her eyes out!"

Father: "But what are you going to do instead, Son?"

Son: "I'm going to leave her alone, but she'd better not start something like that again or I'm going to punch her out!"

Father: "I'm glad you know that you are to leave her alone, and I appreciate your assurance that you are going to keep your hands and your feet to yourself. Thank you very much."

The father then walks away without expressing any anger or frustration either in what he says or how he postures himself.

In this entire encounter, the father never allowed himself to get dragged into the bottomless pit of trying to figure out what is fair and who is to blame. No vain attempt was made to answer unanswerable questions. With empathy and understanding, he acknowledged the boy's anger and frustration, each time reiterating his expectation of the direction the boy's behavior is to take, then invited the boy to describe how he should behave even when angry. Self-instruction is a powerful teacher.

Thus far, the behavior has been stopped and redirected. But the complete power of this strategy is not realized until the redirected behavior has been reinforced. To do this, the father should wait a minute or so, and then, if the child behaves appropriately, the father should acknowledge that casually, briefly, and descriptively: "Thank you, Son, for being in such good control of your behavior. That's super. You're helping make the home a more comfortable place." Then the father would pat the child on the back, or in some other appropriate way make positive physical contact.

To help you keep your children's behavior in its proper perspective and to help you respond to it appropriately, I suggest that, using the form in Table 1, you categorize their behavior as Appropriate, Inconsequential/Annoying, and Consequential. Since past behavior is the best predictor of future behavior, that will be relatively easy to do. The reminder at the bottom of each column will help you remember how you should respond.

Appropriate	Inconsequential/Annoying	Consequential
Completes homework Does chores Plays nicely with the baby Says please and thank you Is happy Feeds the dog without being asked And so on	Whines Complains Tantrums And so on	Hits to hurt Is verbally mean, ugly, profane Cuts classes at school Refuses to do homework And so on
Acknowledge these behaviors in some positive, reinforcing way	Politely ignore; with empathy, as necessary: "I am sorry you're upset."	Use the stop, redirect, reinforce strategy

Table 1: Categorizing Behavior

Treating more serious types of consequential behavior goes beyond the scope of this book, but is covered in considerable detail in my book *The Power of Positive Parenting: A Wonderful Way To Raise Children*. That book was recently recognized by a panel of professional, certified behavior analysts "as a prototype for clearly and effectively communicating to parents the foundation for creating and maintaining a behaviorally safe and healthy home, thereby eliminating the motivation for children to display behavior problems, and plainly and accurately explaining 'how to solve' the behavior problems most commonly found in homes."

For most consequential behaviors, however, by anticipating them, preparing responses in advance, then practicing those responses, the vast, vast majority of those behaviors can be handled on the spot without additional help. For example, suppose that a consequential behavior finds a child being verbally assaultive toward a parent. The child might say something like: "You are the worst person I've ever met. You are fat, ugly, and smell bad. I hate you with a passion!" An appropriate *pro*active response would go like this:

Parent: "I'm sorry you feel that way, but I'm more sorry that you would allow your anger to take control of you."

Child: "My anger is not out of control. *You* are. Your entire life is out of control. As a parent you are totally lacking."

Parent: "Regardless of how you feel about me personally, attacking me this way does not speak well of you."

Child: "I hate it when you try to sidestep the realities of your own inadequacies with those little word games you play."

Parent: "That aside, what would be a more mature way for a person your age to handle anger?"

At this point, the child would most probably do one of four things: (1) Stomp off in a huff, in which event the parent would go on about his/her business; (2) Lash back with another ugly verbal barrage, in which event the parent would say, simply and briefly: "I know how you feel. I hope you're feeling better soon." Then smile and go to other things. Great care must be taken to put an end to such interaction after only three, and no more than four, verbal exchanges; (3) Respond, at least, to some level of decency and appropriateness: "I know what you're after. You want me to keep all this ugly truth to myself," in which event the parent would say, "Thank you," smile, then leave; (4) Refuse to drop it; refuse to let it go. Should this happen, the following illustration describes a response that many parents have found effective, and which provides a framework within which parents can tailor an effective response to almost any explosive, persistent situation:

Child: "Don't give me that #@&!!! You're darn right I'm angry, and for good reason. I'm not leaving until my demands are met! Do you understand that? I am not leaving until . . . !'"

Parent: (calmly, firmly, and looking directly into the child's eyes) "Having heard you state your position on this matter several times, I am confident I know exactly what your concerns are. But since emotions are so high, I refuse to discuss them now. We will have to wait until things have calmed down."

Child: "No! No! No! I will not wait."

Parent: "What do you have to gain or lose by keeping this up?"

         (**Note**: Don't tell the child. Have the child tell you.)

Child: "What I have to gain or lose is beside the point."

Parent: "Before being too sure about that, take a few minutes to think it over. You have an important date coming up and you'll want to use the car. Give this some thought. I've given as much time to this matter as it deserves."

(**Note**: Toss into the conversation a few glimpses of reality—the kinds of things children often lose sight of when their perception of reality is obscured by the smoke generated by the fire of their own emotions; then calmly, politely, and deliberately proceed to other things.)

You might be saying to yourself, "This will never work with my kid. You *don't* know *my* kid." Well, don't be too sure about that. Remember, behavior is largely a product of its immediate environment. Fix the environment, and you fix the behavior. Rarely does volatile, angry, mouthy behavior persist for long in a calm, composed, serene environment. You'll just have to believe me on that. But I know what I'm talking about. I've been there many times and it has *never* failed me. And why? Because it's based on good solid science. Do it—you'll be glad you did. If it doesn't work, let me know. For that matter, let me know if it does work. I love to share parents' successes with other parents.

If the parent will practice prepared, proactive responding, the child will learn quickly that pursuing the matter is getting nowhere. So why go on? In the absence of any parental attempt to defend oneself, get to the bottom of things, or to make some brilliant point using logic and reason—all of which simply make matters worse—the matter is soon put to rest. As hard to believe as it might seem, it really does work well most of the time, which is about the best you can hope for under the circumstances.

To help deal with predictable outbursts of ugly anger, I have many parents using the tool found in Table 2. Well in advance of the problem, I have parents anticipate, based on past behavior, what a child might say or do. I then have the parent prepare a "proactive" response; a calm reasonable response that keeps the lines of communication open between the parent and the child. They then let the consequences—positive or negative—deliver the message. In the long run, it's the best way to go.

The Predictable Behavior	A "Proactive" Response
My teenage son will tell me he doesn't care if he passes or fails in school, and refuses to do his homework. He will say, "School is dumb. I hate it. I'll do just fine without it."	"Sometimes school and homework can be a drag. I hope you'll rethink your decision. "Obviously I can't, nor will I try to, force you to do well in school. That's up to you. "You're upset now. Before you close the door on this matter, give it some serious thought. Perhaps we can discuss it later. I love you."

Table 2. Preparing for Inappropriate Consequential Behavior

These preparations must be done well in advance, and practiced. If you wait until the crisis occurs before deciding what to do, you're a goner. You *must* be prepared well in advance. Since past behavior is the best predictor of future behavior, the chances are very good that you'll be able to prepare well in advance and be ready for the crisis.

. . . .

Not being prepared makes you vulnerable. Remember, you are mature and highly civilized. A child is not. A child will say and do things to you that you'd never dream of saying or doing to your parents (though as a child you might have!). That's just garden variety, age-typical, weed behavior. As the seasons of our lives change, the weeds die out, giving way to the fruit we have worked so hard to produce. The harvest will come.

As I have studied and observed the route to maturity, civility, and selflessness, I have observed that it looks very much like that illustrated in Figure 7. It moves upward steadily until the onset of puberty. Once into adolescence, it tends to take a dip, typically making the years $13\frac{1}{2}$ to $17\frac{1}{2}$ about the worst parenting years of all. It is during these years that children have mouths and bodies that are capable of adult-like behavior, but the maturity and civility to match them are yet to be learned. Being so far out of sync, the organism becomes capable of some pretty bizarre, rude, and ugly behaviors. Invincibility seems only natural, parents become insufferably stupid ("without a life"), and mortality becomes boundless. It's like putting a loaded gun in the hands of a five-year-old. He's able to shoot it, but too inexperienced to know of its danger or its uses, so the bullets fly around aimlessly. If there was ever a time when parents need to be close to their children, involved, and visible, this is the time. It is their last great window of opportunity, as documented so clearly by the Resnick study (Resnick, 1997) of adolescent behavior, and parents' influence on it, which I cited earlier.

In Strategy No. 4 I discuss eight traps parents get themselves caught in that tend to lessen their positive, long-term influence on their children. But before addressing them I want to discuss the dangers of what I call "behavioral noise," and how it can put wedges between parents and their children. I address this now because it is so often the thing that lures parents into the traps from which they have such difficulty escaping.

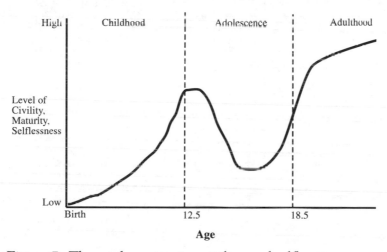

Figure 7: The road to maturity, civility, and selflessness.

Behavioral noise refers to the low-level civility of things kids do and say that reflect their frustrations and anger of the moment. They are outlandish, typically stated in absolute terms ("You *always* give him what he wants," "I can *never* do anything right," "You're the *worst* mother who ever lived" and so on), and are generally accompanied by a lot of huffing and puffing and stomping about. It can be quite a scene. Just remember, it's almost always just "noise."

As parents, we err when we take all of that foolishness literally, believe it, or allow ourselves to be intimidated by it. For the most part it's nothing more than spectacular, energized blustering, and it should be viewed by parents as more of an outlandish vaudeville act than as serious theater.

Table 3 gives several examples of behavioral noise, followed by how to either get trapped by it, or remain calm and composed above it.

Behavioral Noise	Getting Trapped	Remaining Safe
"He started it!"	"You're always blaming someone else! Well, Buddy, it isn't going to work this time!"	"Perhaps he did. I'm sorry. Nevertheless what do I expect of you, even if someone else starts it?"
"I hate you. You're the worst mother/father who ever lived. I'd rather have been born as shark bait than as your kid!"	"Shark bait, huh. Sounds like exactly what you deserve! My heart goes out to the shark. P.S. You're not so loveable yourself, Sweetie!"	"You're very upset. Perhaps you have reason to be upset. We'll talk about it when our emotions are calm."
"You never listen to a word I say. Talking to you is like talking to a tree stump."	"When you talk to me, I wish I were a tree stump."	"I'll take that as a hint and make sure I don't appear uninterested. Thanks."
"I can't wait to get out of this dump; this hell hole."	"Well, at least we share one wish in common."	"I can imagine that sometimes it does feel pretty confining to be at home. I think that's quite natural."
"You don't love me, and that really hurts."	"Honey, I love you so much. Surely you know that. How can you possibly feel that way given all I do for you?"	"I'm sorry you feel that way, Dear. Let's work on that together."

Table 3: Avoiding the Behavioral Noise Trap

Behavioral noise is all about us. We observe it in traffic by people who shake their fists at other drivers, yell out their disgust, honk their horns at the slightest annoyance . . . well, you know what I mean. We see it at supermarket checkouts by mouthy, angry people annoyed at a slow customer, an inept clerk, or a delay in service. We get trapped when we react, in kind, to such "noise."

I had an experience recently in which reacting in kind to behavioral noise could have gotten me into a heap of trouble. I was traveling to a speaking assignment in California, my plane was late, and it was well after lunch time before I found a restaurant where I could get a meal.

After placing my order I took a seat at a corner table, and without realizing it settled into a bit of a trance as I stared off into space. I was startled out of my lethargy by a big, angry fellow who bellowed, "What are you staring at, Buddy!?" I shook my head a bit, as if to clear away the cobwebs of semiconsciousness, only to realize that this fellow had entered the field of my glassy gaze, and it appeared to him as though I was staring at him. Happily—or I should say, fortunately for me—I had enough wits about me to not get trapped by either trying to answer his angry question, or become defensive. The guy could have broken me in two like a matchstick. I took the safe route.

Me: "I'm sorry. I was unaware that I appeared to be staring. I'm quite tired, having just arrived in town after a long delayed plane ride. If I offended you, I'm truly sorry and I apologize."

Him: (Stunned, quiet, and somewhat embarrassed at his boisterousness) "Oh. No problem. Forget it. My mistake," as he quietly walked away.

I felt really good at the results, and was reminded once again of the long-term benefits of responding in a safe way to behavioral noise. Believe me, being able to walk out of that restaurant with both of us happy was a lot better than being carried out on a stretcher, beaten to a pulp by some very big, very angry fellow—which is what happens in one form or another, thousands of times a day, all over the face of the earth: getting trapped by the noise, reacting in kind, then experiencing severe though avoidable consequences.

Now a word about traps.

Strategy No. 4: Avoid Parent Traps

As I have worked with families, I have been impressed at the misguided efforts parents frequently make in their desperate attempts at managing their children's behavior. A careful analysis of these desperate efforts has revealed what I have chosen to call "Parenting Traps." Following is a brief discussion of the eight most common traps. Remember, our job as parents is to create an environment in which the general level of positive reinforcement is high, thus raising the chances that inappropriate behavior will be low. Avoiding these eight traps will be of inestimable help in that regard.

Trap 1: Criticism

Verbally berating children because they don't perform well is no incentive whatsoever *to* perform well; rather, it simply heightens the child's sense of inadequacy and dampens any desire to improve behavior (escape and avoidance). Under the guise of "constructive criticism" parents fool no one. Statements like the following have virtually no value at all: "I simply can't understand why you didn't do better on that examination. We all know that you have the ability if you would just apply yourself. Is it too much to ask you to simply do as well as you know you can?"

Here the parent is simply lashing out in frustration, and the child knows very well that what was said was simply a thinly veiled tongue-lashing by a concerned but angry, desperate, out-of-control parent.

Rather than using criticism, parents should genuinely express their concern for the child's well-being, restate their expectations of the child, and then manage contingencies which in turn manage the behavior. For example:

Parent: "Honey, we just want you to know that we are concerned about your success at school, and hope you'll do your best."

Child: "I am doing my best. What more do you want out of me?"

Parent: "We expect you to apply yourself and take your studies seriously. What do we mean when we say 'apply yourself?'"

Child: (Disgusted) "I know what you mean! You want me to get my dumb homework done and handed in. I hate that class. The teacher is a number one jerk. It's so boring."

Parent: "Right on! Getting your homework done and handed in on time will be a great first step. What else can you do?"

Note: The parent made no mention of "dumb homework," the teacher as a "jerk," or the "boring" class. All of that is simply behavioral noise. Ignore it. The parent's attention was focused *entirely* on getting the homework done and handed in.

Child: "I don't know."

Parent: "When exam time rolls around, what can you do
         to prepare for the exam?"

         Note: Parents should never tell a child something
         he/she already knows; rather, they should create a
         setting in which the child is invited, free of risk, to
         do the telling.

Child: "Study. I know, study. What a waste of time study-
         ing for that dumb class!"

Parent: "You are exactly correct! Study is the key. And
         when you do these things, Honey, that is, do your
         homework, hand it in, and study for your exams,
         really valuable privileges will be yours. What are
         some of these privileges?"

         Note: At this point consequences for compliance
         or non-compliance are discussed, as per the
         Premack Principle (Jenson, Sloane, and Young,
         1988, p. 67). That is, once the less desirable task is
         completed (study/homework), desirable privileges
         (TV, use of the car, and so on) will be forthcom-
         ing. It's Grandma's Law: Eat your vegetables and
         you can have pie and ice cream.

This puts the responsibility to perform where it should be:
on the child. The responsibility of the parent is to create
an environment that will give the child reason to perform
as well as he or she is able to so that positive benefits will
follow.

During a twenty-year study of schooling, I visited ran-
domly selected schools and classrooms in all fifty states, all
of America's territories and protectorates, and fourteen for-
eign countries (Latham, 1997). As a part of that study, I

. . . .

asked hundreds of students, "Why do you do the school-work you are assigned?" Virtually without exception they told me, "Because if I don't, I'm in trouble." (Precisely the same response I get from children at home when they are asked a similar question, as I noted earlier. This is that old, lingering, ugly matter of behaving well only to avoid the negative consequences of behaving badly, rather than behaving well to enjoy the positive consequences of doing so.)

When criticized for not doing as well as he or she could or should, what are the chances of the child saying: "Thank you. I needed that. From this point on I will do my level best, even when I don't want to." Get the idea?

Trap 2: Sarcasm

As with criticism, sarcasm has absolutely no healthy quality about it whatsoever. It is a desperate attempt to manage behavior in the absence of skills or competence. Calling a child a "sissy," or using words like "cute" and "pretty boy" often serve no purpose other than to degrade a child and put distance between that child and his or her parent(s). A fifteen-year-old boy recently told me, "My parents are always reminding me that I'm not dumb; I'm smart enough to get into trouble all the time."

Parents typically use sarcasm, thinly veiled as humor, hoping it will function as something of a shock treatment that will help make a point they haven't been able to make in the past. But parents need to understand, unequivocally, that such statements do not deliver any kind of useful message or provide any incentive whatsoever for the child to behave better. They are nothing more nor less than coercive statements that encourage their children to escape and avoid the coercer, and ultimately behave even worse.

Trap 3: Threats

Threats tend to be useless and counterproductive for at least three reasons. First, they are thoughtless, vacuous statements blurted out in moments of anger; second, they are almost never carried out because they are typically so outlandish that they couldn't be carried out even if the parents wanted to; and third, they cause parents a lot of quandary as they try to wiggle out of the trap they get themselves into.

For example, consider this: In a rage, the parent shouts, "Okay, buster. You did it this time. You are grounded for six months. Do you understand?! Six months! No car, no TV, no allowance, no nothing." Then off the parent stomps, flushed with anger, breathing heavily—and half an hour later saying to himself/herself: "You idiot! How are you going to get out of this mess? Will you ever learn?"

An effective antidote to threat-making is for the parent to stop, take a couple of deep breaths, and say, "I fear that I might handle this situation badly if I proceed feeling as I do. Excuse me for a few minutes while I regain my composure. I'll be back soon." The parent then retires to a quiet, secure place, calms down, practices a proactive response, returns, and says, "Now, regarding this matter, it is obvious that your behavior has earned some unpleasant consequences. We need to discuss those now." The parent then proceeds proactively.

The results of such a calm, deliberate, positive, proactive response is generally startlingly effective, and the exercise of self-control modeled by the parent will, with considerable certainty, have a profound, instructive effect on the child's ability to proactively handle anger and stress in his/her own life. Rather than using threats, parents should focus on applying earned consequences that (1) are given free of anger, (2) clearly state what will follow, and (3) are carried out as stated. Again (for emphasis), consequences must be reasonable and fit the offense.

Trap 4: Logic

Using logic is typically an ill-fated attempt to make adult wisdom attractive to a child, and seldom works. I have yet to have a parent tell me something like this: "Upon my explaining things logically to my child, my child said to me, 'Mother, what a powerful point you have just made! I can now clearly see the error in my thinking. From this day forward, I will make certain that my behavior is guided by your wise and mature counsel.'"

More likely, children will counter adult logic with statements like: "Oh, you just don't know what you're talking about. Get real!" To them, it is not wisdom of the ages, it is wisdom of the aged, and children just don't identify with it. Parents are well advised to save their breath rather than be tempted to use logic as a behavior management tool.

It is certainly appropriate in moments of calm to use logic to explain a situation or to help a child understand why something happened or will happen in the future. If used in this way, I caution that it be done when the child is calm and able to be reasoned with.

. . . .

Trap 5: Arguing

Since we already know that arguing is a totally and absolutely ineffective way of managing children's behavior, I'll not spend time rehashing it here. As some wise observer once noted, "Arguing with a kid is like wrestling with a pig. They both get dirty but the pig loves it."

There is, however, a form of arguing that is so subtle that parents don't even realize they are arguing; rather, they see themselves as being compassionate and concerned. Therefore, I call it "Compassionate Arguing," but it is arguing nonetheless. It goes like this:

Child: "I just don't have any friends. I must be the ugliest kid in school."

Parent: "Now, now, you're not ugly at all. You're a fine looking individual and you have every reason to be proud of who you are."

Child: "No, I am not attractive and I don't have any reason to be proud of myself. If I was as good as you say I am, I'd have more friends than I'd know what to do with. You know as well as I do that I don't have any friends."

Parent: "What do you mean you don't have any friends? You have friends over at the house all the time. You obviously have a whole lot more going for you than you think you do."

Child: "Hey, who you *think* my friends are and who I *want* to be my friends are two different things. If you knew how things really were in my life, *you'd* know I'm as ugly as *I* know I'm ugly!"

In such an exchange, we observe an interesting varia-tion to arguing. The parent is arguing in behalf of the child—which the child rejects; and the child is arguing in behalf of his or her own perceived inadequacies—which the parent rejects. But no matter how the encounter is analyzed, the end result is that everything the parent is saying and everything the child is saying simply reinforce the child's perception of his/her sense of inadequacy. The child, in fact, is arguing in *defense* of his/her perceived inadequacy!

However it is structured, arguing is counterproductive.

Trap 6: Questioning

Parents are forever questioning children about their inappropriate behavior: "Why did you hit your sister?" "What in the world are you doing?" "How many times am I going to have to tell you to stop that?" and so on. Unless parents need information to help solve a problem, they should never—I repeat, *never*—ask a child a question about his or her inappropriate behavior. There are three reasons for this. First, questioning a child about his or her inappropriate behavior typically encourages the child to lie, be evasive, or be defensive. Such questioning tends to be threatening, and at the time lying can seem to be a very easy and convenient way to get out of a hot spot. Or the child will be evasive: "He started it! It's not my fault." Or the child will be defensive: "Why do you always pick on me?"

Second, when parents ask children questions about

their inappropriate behavior they don't want an answer so much as they want compliance—or an assurance of compliance in the future—and an answer, whether it's true or not, satisfies neither. In fact an answer is virtually never accepted. For example, consider the following scenario:

Parent: "Why did you hit your sister?"
Child: "I hit my sister because she is ugly, and I was only trying to fix her face."

The child answered the question. Did the answer provide the parent with any information that would help solve a problem? How likely is it, for example, that the parent would answer by saying, "Oh, I see. Yes, you are correct. Your sister is ugly and we certainly should do something about that. I'm glad you have called that to my attention, and we'll get right busy on it." Such a response, obviously, is as absurd as the child's answer.

Did the answer provide any assurance that the child would no longer hit his sister? How likely is it that the father would respond by saying something like, "Very well, Son. It was perfectly okay for you to hit your sister that time if you can assure me that you have gotten that out of your system and you will never hit your sister again." Another absurd answer to a dumb question.

Parents virtually never ask children questions about their inappropriate behavior for any constructive or problem-solving purpose. They ask questions because at the moment it is a handy way of blowing off steam. Unfortunately, in the final analysis it makes the relationship between the parent and the child worse rather than better.

The third reason why one should never ask a child a

question about his or her inappropriate behavior is that it simply directs a lot of parental attention to inappropriate behavior; hence increasing the probability that inappropriate behavior will reoccur in the future. Again, parents should *never* ask a child a question about his or her inappropriate behavior unless they *really* need information to solve problems. When two of my children were young, the older of the two fed his younger sister a bottle of baby aspirin. The question, "How much aspirin did she eat?" was reasonable because it made it possible for us as parents to determine whether or not our daughter needed to have her stomach pumped—which it turned out was necessary. To have asked our son, "Why did you feed your sister those aspirin?" would have only delayed treatment. (By the way, we had to have both their stomachs pumped. Good use of natural consequences.)

A mother wrote to me, "I cringe to think that I have asked my daughter, 'Would you like a spanking?' What a stupid question. What was the child going to say? 'Sure, Mom, I love spankings. I'm a member of the young masochists' club.'"

Trap 7: Force: Verbal or Physical

Coercive attempts at managing behavior evidence themselves in the use of physical or verbal force more than in any other way, and the results are predictable: an inclination on the part of children to avoid, escape, and/or countercoerce. When using force, parents of young children plant the seeds for misery that will certainly come into full bloom during adolescence (Walker et al., 1989).

Parents can get away with using force when their children are young, but when the children get older it becomes increasingly less effective, more divisive, and can effectively destroy all bonds between parents and their children. In this regard, my advice to parents is simple: Unless what you are about to say or do to your child has a high probability for making things better, don't say it and don't do it.

No hitting, squeezing, grabbing, jerking, shaking, or shouting. I could easily triple the size of this book with a review of the long-range disastrous effects of the use of verbal or physical force as means of compelling children to behave well. Just don't do it. The more parents hit, the worse children behave. The louder parents shout, the less children listen, and the worse they behave. It is predictable.

Trap 8: Despair, Pleading, Hopelessness

Consider this frequently heard parental lament to a noncompliant child: "I just don't know what I am going to do with you. I have tried everything I know. I am simply out of ideas. I don't have the foggiest notion what it's going to take to get you to shape up. Do you have any ideas?" What is the parent to expect from something like this? Obviously, the parent isn't looking for an answer. Recalling Trap 6, how likely is it that the child would say: "Well, Mother, as a matter of fact I do have some suggestions for you. I have been spending some time in the library reading in the behavioral literature and there are some distinct possibilities there for improving your parenting skills. If you would like, I would be more than happy to discuss that literature with you in depth, and between the two of us I am sure we can figure out a way of shaping me up while at the same time making you a competent parent." Believe me, if a kid came back with a response like that he or she had better be out of arms length of the parent, otherwise the encounter could degenerate from verbal to physical— fast.

Obviously, comments like this do nothing more than convince children that their parents are incompetent and do not know how to raise children. A simple, easy-to-apply mixture of empathy, understanding, directiveness, and consequences can keep parents from being trapped. It goes like this:

Parent: "I'm sorry you chose to behave that way. I assume that at the moment you regarded that to be a reasonable option even though, looking back on it, it was obviously a poor choice. What would have been a better way of responding?"

Child: "I did exactly what I wanted to. I hate my sister, and I want to hit her every chance I get."

Parent: "It's obvious to me, Son, that that's what you want to do. But what *should* you do?"

Child: "Well, you expect me to leave her alone."

Parent: "Correct, Son. That's an excellent answer. I appreciate that mature response. I expect you to keep your hands to yourself even in instances where your sister makes you angry. Now, I'd like you to show me what you are going to do in the future if your sister annoys you and you feel like hitting her. Walk across the room and pretend that your sister is near you, has done something to annoy you, and you feel like hitting her. Show me what you're going to do."

Child: (The child walks across the room and role plays walking away from his imaginary sister.) "I suppose that's what you want me to do."

Parent: "Correct, Son. That is exactly what you should do. You have just demonstrated to me what you will do in the future. You will simply walk away without hitting your sister or saying mean things to her. Furthermore, Son, when you do control yourself that way and just walk away from your sister rather than hitting her or being mean, you will earn some very valuable privileges. What are some things around the house that you really enjoy doing?"

Child: "Do you mean to tell me that if I hit that stupid sister of mine I'm not going to be able to play with my Nintendo?"

Parent: "Okay, Nintendo is one of those privileges you enjoy. What other privileges are there here at the house you enjoy a lot?"

Child: "Well, I like riding my bicycle, and I like watching television, and I'm also glad that I get an allowance."

Note: Inviting the child to identify privileges he or she really enjoys is the best way to identify what consequences are the most valuable to the child, and will likely have the greatest effect on managing the behavior (Jenson, Sloane, and Young, p. 67).

Parent: "I would agree with that, Son. I've noticed that

those things really are important to you, and I want you to know, absolutely, that if you choose to manage your behavior well—and what do I mean when I say 'manage your behavior well?'"

Child: "It means that I won't hit my sister. That I'll just walk away." (As he mutters under his breath, "I hate my sister. I wish she'd die.")

Parent: "Right, Son, that's exactly what I expect you to do: to manage your own behavior, which means not hitting your sister. And when you do manage your own behavior well, what privileges will you earn?"

Note: The emphasis should be on "earned privileges." The child must learn that there are no "noncontingent reinforcers." No free lunch.

Child: "I know what you mean, Dad. You'll let me ride my bike and play my Nintendo and all that stuff."

Parent: "That's right, Son. You will earn the privilege of having those things when you want them. And that's wonderful! On the other hand, Son, should you fail to manage your behavior well—and what do I mean when I say *fail* to manage your behavior well?"

Child: "Well, it means I hit my dumb sister."

Parent: "Right. You'd hit your sister. If you do that, what privileges will you deny yourself?"

Child: "I know what you're talking about, Dad."

Parent: "So, Son, what can I expect of you in the future when your sister annoys you?"

Child: "I guess I'd better leave her alone and just hope that she gets run over by a school bus."

Parent: "I'm glad you understand my expectations, Son."

. . . .

Note: It is important that all of the noisy, age-typical, garden variety, weed behaviors such as "I hate my sister," "My dumb sister," "I hope she gets run over by a school bus," are noisy inconsequential behaviors that should just be put on extinction. Remember, attention should never be given to a behavior that is not to be repeated, unless it is a consequential behavior to be treated therapeutically as was discussed earlier.

Also, when the parent's countenance falls, that's when the carnage begins. That's when the hitting and shouting starts. That's when the door is flung open for abuse. Parents who abuse their children, beat on them, argue with them, shout at them and threaten them, are not smiling. Keep smiling.

Chapter Four
. . . .

Drugs, Classics, and Consequences

A Word About Treating Behavior with Drugs

Volumes have been written, and will continue to be written, about the pros and cons of using drugs to help control behavior. Before *any* type of drug-based treatment is used, careful attention *must* be given to the following:

1. Consistent with the focus of this book, create an environment in your home that properly shapes behavior in the first place. (For additional help see the suggested readings at the end of this book.) Remember, behavior is largely a product of its immediate environment. Fix the environment and you are well on your way to fixing the behavior.

   In that regard, I caution you to limit television viewing *of any kind*! As reported by one researcher, TV puts the brain into "hibernation," and the only things that keep it awake are repeated startle effects in the form of violence and rapidly changing visual and auditory stimulation. He further noted that before age four years old, such stimuli actually alters the normal growth and development of brain tissue, making the brain less able to handle more complex

. . . .
71

tasks common to the academic demands of schooling and socially challenging situations. Furthermore, it makes kids "hyper" (Pierce, January 14, 1998). ADD/ADHD can easily become the bitter fruits of such super-hyper environments.

2. Carefully analyze behaviors of concern, as described in this book, then proceed with care and caution. In other words, don't be too quick to assume the worst. I recall an experience in the family of our youngest son. His oldest daughter returned home from her first day of school with a list of behaviors her parents should watch for; behaviors which were supposedly indicative of ADD/ADHD. Our son read through the list then exclaimed, "Dad, this describes me to a 'T' as a boy."

   In my work with families, I see this repeatedly: otherwise healthy, rambunctious kids exhibiting annoying, noisy, age-typical behavior being classified as behaviorally dysfunctional when, in fact, they are just kids behaving as kids behave.

   A mother told me recently of how grateful she was that some years earlier I had advised her to not medicate her son's behavior. She said: "I just rode the tide. Parenting isn't easy. And now I am so glad I did because he is a fine, healthy, in-control young man."

   Drugging behavior, characterized by one of my colleagues as "improving the quality of life with chemicals," is risky business and must be done with the utmost care. A junior high school teacher lamented to me about one of his students who, during a bout of inappropriate behavior, protested, "I can't be expected to behave. I forgot to take my Ritalin this morning."

3. Make absolutely certain that it is the *child's* mental and behavioral well-being that are being treated. I am simply astounded by the number of distressed parents who complain "I can't take it any longer" when describing their child's behavior; the implication being, "Fix this kid so I can be comfortable."

   True, as parents our mental health is important, and a well-behaved child is certainly more comfortable to raise than is a behaviorally challenging child. Still it is the well-being of the child that should be the major concern.

4. Make certain that the behavior really is beyond the limits of "normal"; that thorough, respected testing has been done to establish that the behavior is in need of special attention.

   A mother (one of many) was recently in my office. She told me her son was ADHD and on Ritalin. I asked her how this diagnosis had been made. She answered: "I described his behavior to my pediatrician. He told me my son was ADHD and put him on Ritalin."

   I asked what testing had been done and whether any reference had been made to the descriptors of ADHD found in the *Diagnostic Statistical Manual of Mental Disorders*. She said nothing of that sort was done. The doctor never saw the child, nor did he reference any diagnostic criteria to support his prescribed treatment. This, folks, is behavior mismanagement.

Drugging behavior is risky business. Furthermore, no matter how good the drug, how accurately it is prescribed, or how properly it is administered, it *must never be the only treatment of choice!* Behavioral treatment must *always* be a prominent part of any treatment package aimed at serving behavior (Flora, 1998). Don't ever forget that. Parents are derelict in their duty if they turn the treatment of a child's challenging or dysfunctional behavior over to a pill.

Remember, medicines and drugs are used to treat diseases. Behavior in any form is not a disease (Miller and Brown, 1997). To treat maladaptive behavior solely with drugs is tantamount to treating a compound fracture solely with faith. Let us be crystal clear about the irresponsibility of that.

A Word About Class(ics)

A casual look at and listen to the contemporary scene brings us to no other conclusion than that we live in a culturally trashy world. Music, TV, the Internet, movies, magazines, the tabloids, talk shows — you name it — seem to be competing for that which can sink the deepest into the muck and mire of filth and depravity. As one commentator noted, "Think up the most disturbing, vile, perversely twisted act you can imagine—and chances are it's got a news group and two dozen web-sites" (Jones, 1998).

True, parents can't shield their children from all of this, but they can keep it out of their homes, or at least keep it to a minimum, and they can surely replace it with a touch of class (and they'd better!). Consider the following as it addresses each of these two important parenting responsibilities.

. . . .

Minimizing the Trash at Home

Children must know that home is a refuge from the slings and arrows of the world; that it is a safe place. They might not agree with their parents about what is or isn't safe, but that's okay. They don't have to agree, they only have to understand.

Suppose that a child brings into the home a piece of music, a video, a magazine—whatever, you know what I mean—and you have decided that giving expression to it in your home compromises the "safety" of your home. In such an event, you must take a stand, prohibit its having unrestricted expression in your home, and be prepared for a huge amount of very noisy protest. It would very likely go like this:

Parent: "I know you want to listen to that CD in the house, but that stuff is not acceptable here. I'm asking you to not play it in our house."

Child: "What do you mean, you don't want me to play it in the house. This is hot stuff. I'll listen to it in my bedroom whether you want me to or not."

Parent: "Son, I know this will make you very, very angry, but how angry you get is beside the point. The point is that stuff is vile and not acceptable in this home."

Note: Avoid any discussion about how "hot" the stuff is, or whether you can or can't stop him. Stay with the importance of protecting the general quality of the environment in the home against filthy, vile, wretched stuff.

Child: "Dad, nobody in the house will hear it. I'll be

wearing my earphones. And my door will be closed. You're making a big deal over nothing."

Parent: "You'll hear it, Son, and that's what worries me. You are an important somebody to me. Very important. Why do I worry about your listening to that stuff?"

Note: Stay completely away from how big a deal it is. The probability is zero of your being able to convince the boy that the stuff is bad for him.

Child: "I told you, Dad, it's not as terrible as you think. It isn't turning me into a monster, you know."

Parent: "Thank you for the assurance that it is not having a negative effect on you. Nevertheless, what do you understand my position to be?"

Child: "You want me to not listen to this. You are afraid it's going to mess up my life forever. Well, you're wrong. And I'm *going* to listen to it!"

Parent: "Thank you. It is important to me to know that you understand perfectly what my concerns are. I have a serious responsibility to make this home a safe refuge for my family, safe from the vile and wretched things of the world. I'll appreciate your cooperation and help in that regard.

Then you leave it at that. The boy now knows three very important things (1) He knows your expectations. Research in adolescent behavior has taught us of the long-term importance of that (Resnick, et al., 1997). Whether he complies is another thing. That's his choice. But he needs to know what is expected of him. (2) He knows you care about him and about the general well-being of the home. Knowing that will have a powerful effect on how he regards the home, and about how he should behave in it. It *will* have a moderating effect. (3) It clearly establishes the role of the parent as the head of and leader in the home. The home needs a leader who has a clearly established set of values and expectations. When they become adults, our children's homes will tend to reflect that.

Parents, guard against the attempts of your children to intimidate you with loud, bombastic, pretentious behavior. (For a thorough treatment of this, I refer you to my book *The Power of Positive Parenting*, pp. 283–97.) You must be the undisputed head of your home. Your home is *not* a democracy. If you want absolute chaos in your home and family, turn it into a democracy where everyone's vote carries the same weight. No! Your home must be a *gently*, *carefully*, and *lovingly* managed patriarchy or a matriarchy (the kind of home that is managed in the way described here).

That, along with the quality of entertainment acceptable there, will give your home a touch of class that will make it an unusually safe and loving place.

Begin with a Class Act

During a recent phone conversation with one of our daughters, the subject of contemporary music came up. Her oldest daughter is getting to the age where children are being lured into that cesspool of filth and poison. To guard against that happening, from the time her children were born she has introduced them to, and surrounded them with, musical and literary classics. The children have acquired a taste and a value for these fine things. She told us of her and her daughter hearing a contemporary song on the car radio, one that was so characteristic of such trash (I refuse to call it music): loud, profane, obscene, ugly. We are happy that our granddaughter was as repulsed by it as was her mother. Our daughter said something to us that I wish could be said by all parents of young children: "Mom and Dad, I'm so thankful that when Mallory goes to bed at night she is choosing to listen to *Phantom of the Opera*, *The Sound of Music*, and *Rigoletto*."

Children's appetites for music and arts are acquired; they are learned. Parents must do their best to teach the finer things of life to their children. This does not mean that their children will never acquire some appetite for trash, because they likely will. After all, the lure and allure of the world's worst can be alarmingly attractive to youth. But at least this will be counterbalanced by the good and finer things of life. And balance is so very important.

It thrills my wife and me as we go into the homes of our grandchildren and see shelves and shelves of good books, parents monitoring and managing TV viewing, and the exposure of our grandchildren to the finer, sweeter, more ennobling influences.

I recall vividly an experience I had in the early sixties. I was teaching special education at a junior high school. Those were the days when the sweet, melodic strains of contemporary music were just beginning to be invaded by the loud, disgusting, indelicate sounds of what opened the floodgates to the sewers of cacophony that have so thoroughly polluted today's recording industry. My students were being drawn to that, and I was concerned. I decided to introduce them to the classics.

As well as focusing on music, I told the stories and

described the settings that inspired some of the world's greatest music. As I played Tchaikovsky's *Romeo and Juliet*, for example, I read the related scenes from Shakespeare's epic play. I directed the students' attention to how masterfully the music portrayed the sword fight on the streets of Verona between the Montagues and the Capulets. The students listened with rapt attention to the words of the play woven into the inspired and inspiring music of the love theme. And so on with Dvorak's *New World Symphony*, Gershwin's *Rhapsody in Blue*, Til Eulenspiegel's *Merry Pranks* by Richard Strauss, and others. The students loved it.

But it didn't end there. To increase the social contacts between my students and the studentbody at large, I turned my classroom into an entertainment and activities center during the lunch hour. Kids could dance, play chess and checkers, compete in a table tennis tournament, and so on. What thrilled me most, however, was when my students would rush into the room, tugging enthusiastically on the hand of a friend, putting on the record player a piece of music we were studying, then saying, "Isn't that beautiful. Let me tell you the story."

My students became so enthusiastic about the musical classics that they wrote a letter to the Director of the Utah Symphony Orchestra, Maurice Abravanel, and invited the Utah Symphony to perform at the junior high school. And you know what? It did.

Children can be taught to value, enjoy, and want the fine, the refined, the classic things of life. Parents, introduce your children to them. Bless your home and family with a touch of class.

A Word About Consequences

Consequences, and how to apply them, remains a major concern of parents. The general impression is that if we just make consequences miserable enough, our kids will avoid them by being good. Not necessarily so. Not by a long shot. There is a better way.

I am going to end this book with a brief discussion of what that better way is, and with the reminder with which I began this book: as parents, we cannot be absolutely certain that what we do "will be absolutely effective with absolutely all children in absolutely any setting." But when we do it right, and in a manner consistent with what research in human behavior has taught us, we remarkably increase the chances that the best results will be forthcoming. Regarding the use of consequences, I strongly suggest that parents avoid being too quick to attach a negative, aversive consequence to an expectation:

Expectation	Aversive Consequences
"You need to get your homework done."	"And if you don't, you are grounded for the rest of the day!"

Under such a circumstance, the only incentive for the child to behave well is to avoid the negative consequence of *not* behaving well. This is coercive and will make homework and schooling something to be hated, avoided, and escaped. Rather, follow a statement of expectations by empathetically and understandingly inviting a response from the child:

Expectations

Mom: "You need to get your homework done."

Child: "Mom! I'll get it done as soon as this show is over."

Mom: "Good. When will that be?"

Child: "In a while, Mom. Don't worry. I'll get my home-work done."

Mom: "I'm glad for the assurance that you'll get it done. Thanks. But I need to know when you'll have it done."

Child: "Before I go to bed, Mom. Before I go to bed. Don't bug me about it."

Mom: "I'm sure you'd like to put it off until bedtime, but that's not acceptable. Supper will be ready by 6:20, and you need to have it done before then. So tell me when, between now and supper, you will begin your homework, and by when you will have it fin-ished. I need to know that now."

Child: "Okay. I'll have it done before supper."

Mom: "Wonderful. When will you need to get started so you'll be done by supper?"

Child: "Mom. Is this all you have to do, to just bug me about homework?"

Mom: "I know this annoys you. Tell me, when will you start your homework?"

Child: "I'll start it in fifteen minutes, Mom! Now are you happy?"

Mom: Super. What time will that be?"

Child: "I can't believe this. I said in fifteen minutes. Can't you tell time, Mom? Fifteen minutes from now is 4:30. I'll start my homework at 4:30. Do I need to send you an E-mail?"

Mom: "Great! Thanks for pinning that down for me. 4:30 it is.

In this scenario, the mother was totally unmoved by the noise: "Don't worry," "Don't bug me," "Is this all you have to do?" "I can't believe this!"

Rather, the mother, despite the child's low-level-of-civility behavior, offered six positive verbal responses: "Good," "thanks," "wonderful," "super," "great," and "thanks."

The key is to get the child to tell you what he/she is supposed to do. Research in the area of compliance has taught us that "high levels of self-instruction correspond with high levels of correct responding . . . [and] produce desired behavior change" (Taylor and O'Reilly, 1997, pp. 43-58). A wonderful letter from a mother in Michigan nicely illustrates that:

> I have a 13-year-old daughter who would argue with the devil himself about the temperature in hell. On this particular day, she was feeling very slighted and angry at me because I was unable to immediately attend to her. When I told her she must wait until some of the after-school chaos died down, she became very angry at me. I hate it here . . . you're a horrible person . . . you don't have time for me . . . you don't take anything that happens to me seriously . . . I hate you, etc.
>
> This was accompanied by arms flailing, feet stomping, a book bag being slammed on the floor! I'm sure you get the picture.
>
> In the old days [meaning before she read my books *The Power of Positive Parenting*, and *What's a Parent to Do?*), I would have risen to the bait, attempted unsuccessfully to

reason with her, question her, explain my situation [all of the traps]. And we would have ended up in a long drawn out angry emotional scene. The *new* me said (glancing at my watch) I'm sorry you feel that way. I'm sure it seems that way to you now. I'll be willing to talk with you in about an hour when things settle down around here. For now, I expect you to go to your room and get your homework started. Now what is it I expect you to do?

She sputtered, Yeah, well . . . I do . . . and they . . . and you . . . but . . .

I said, What do I expect you to do?

She said, But . . . you . . . you . . . you expect me to go to my room and get my homework started. With that, she semi-calmly headed up the stairs to her room, and I *very* calmly left the kitchen (smiling uncontrollably to myself). 48 seconds flat! This stuff works!

I get a steady stream of letters like that from all over the world: "It works!" And the reason it works is because "this stuff" is anchored in science. Science helps us predict the future, to prepare for it, and to create environments within which we can dramatically increase the chances for success for all.

To emphasize and illustrate this important point, I call your attention to Figure 8. Scenario 1 depicts a circumstance in which the only reason a child has for behaving well is to avoid the negative consequences of behaving badly. This is coercive, and typical of parent/child interactions involving an "and if you don't . . ." ultimatum. Under such a circumstance the best that can be hoped for is begrudging, short-term compliance that the parents force on a child. Over time, this becomes an invitation to a child to escape, avoid, and/or countercoerce (get even).

Scenario 2, on the other hand, puts the business of compliance on the child's shoulders, and in such a way as to create an opportunity and a reason for the child to behave well to enjoy the positive consequences of behaving well.

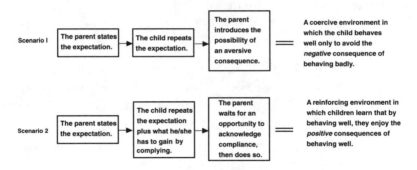

Figure 8. Giving expectations a chance.

These illustrations emphasize the importance of getting the momentum of behavior moving in a positive direction, using noncoercive methods. In this way we create an environment in which children behave well so they can enjoy the positive consequences of behaving well. When that happens, we are safe and our children will ultimately want to be with us and near us.

Though it is absolutely necessary that we make the environment of our home safe and loving for our own children, it is similarly important that we make it safe and loving for our children's friends.

I experienced the truth of this after conducting a self-management workshop for state prison inmates. Most of those in the workshop were sex offenders. After the workshop a young man, a fine-looking fellow who seemed so out of place as an inmate in a state prison, greeted me with a warm handshake. He looked vaguely familiar, but since I meet so many people in so many places I quickly dismissed the possibility of having ever met him, particularly since the prison was not in the state where I lived.

I was taken back when he asked, "How is your daughter?" (whom he identified by name). I was alarmed at the question, but happy to be able to tell him she was fine. He continued, "I doubt you recognize me, since my hair was long then and I dressed weird. I went to high school with your daughter and have been in your home many times. I want you to know, though, that your daughter was never in any danger because of me. I always felt welcome in your home. You and your wife were kind to me despite how awful I must have looked to you. I can imagine how you must have felt having me in your home and a friend of your daughter's. Nevertheless, I was always impressed with how welcome you made me feel, despite how I looked. I can still remember some of the visits I had with you folks. During those visits I came to know of your love and concern for your daughter. That had a great influence on how I treated her. Please give her my regards. Tell her an old friend says hello." And he walked away nameless.

In recalling this experience I must make it clear that parents must be careful to protect their homes from danger. It isn't possible to detail in every imaginable instance how to do that; but as a general rule, make your home a safe and friendly place for your children's friends, as well. The benefits can be immeasurable!

By E-mail, the mother of a "one-time difficult 15-year-old daughter who is in the process of becoming civilized," wrote, after having made her home "safe and friendly for everyone," "suddenly five or six teenage girls descend upon our kitchen, talk, laugh, giggle, and disappear. Isn't it great!"

Conclusion

How children behave is in large measure a function of how well their parents behave. If parents keep doing what they've always done, they will keep getting what they have always gotten. This book has as much to do with improving parents' behavior as it has to do with helping children behave better. Before any attempt is made to "shape up" the way children behave, parents *must* "shape up" their own behavior. Making home a safe and loving place begins with safe, loving, and stable parents.

I close with a poignant message for parents from Kahlil Gibran's book *The Prophet* (New York: Alfred II. Knopf, 1995, p. 18):

> You are the bows from which your children as
>   living arrows are sent forth.
> The archer sees the mark upon the path of the infinite,
>   and he bends you with his might that his arrows
>   may go swift and far.
> Let your bending in the archer's hand be for gladness,
> For even as he loves the arrow that flies,
>   so he loves also the bow that is stable.

References

Bijou, S. W. (1993). *Behavior analysis of child development*. Reno, Nev.: Context Press.

Bijou, S. W. (1988). "Behaviorism: History and Educational Applications." In T. Husen, and T. N. Postlethaite (Eds.), *International Encyclopedia of Education* (pp. 444-51). N.Y.: Pergamon Press.

Cautela, J. R. (1993, March). *General Level of Reinforcement*. Paper presented at the fifth annual meeting of the International Behaviorology Association, Little Compton: R. I.

Colt, G. H. (1996). "The Healing Revolution." *Life*, pp. 86-90.

Cousins, N. (1979). *Anatomy of An Illness As Perceived by the Patient*. N.Y.: Norton.

Daniels, A. (1994). *Bringing Out the Best in People*. San Francisco: McGraw-Hill, Inc.

Eftimiades, M., Goulding, C., Duignan-Cabrera, A., and Podesta, J.S. (June 23, 1997). "Why Are Kids Killing?" *People*, 47 (24), pp. 46-53.

Flora, S. R. (April 10, 1998). "The Debate on Prescription

Privileges for Psychologists: An Opportunity for Behavior Analysis." *Balance*, 4 (1), pp. 2-3.

Gibbs, W. W. (Special Edition/1997). "Seeking the Criminal Element." *Scientific American*, Special Edition: Mysteries of the Mind, pp. 102-10.

Hart, B. and Risley, T. R. (1995). *Meaningful Differences in the Everyday Experience of Young American Children*. Baltimore, Md.: Brookes.

Jenson, W. R., Sloane, H. N, and Young, K. R. (1988). *Applied Behavior Analysis in Education: A Structured Teaching Approach*. Englewood Cliffs, N. J.: Prentice Hall.

Jones, K. (February 5-18, 1998), "Lust in Cyberspace." *The Independent* (St. George, Utah), 2 (16).

Lake, B. G. (December 21, 1997). "Society's Ugly New Attitude: 'You Don't Mind If I'm Rude, Do You?'" *Neighbors*. North Highland, Calif.

Latham, Glenn I. (1944). *The Power of Positive Parenting: A Wonderful Way to Raise Children*. Logan, Utah: P & T ink.

Latham, Glenn I. (1997). *Behind the Schoolhouse Door: Eight Skills Every Teacher Should Have*. Logan, Utah: P & T ink.

Leo, J. (February 1998). It's all relative. *Reader's Digest*.

Lindsley, O. R. (1963). "Geriatric behavioral prosthetics." In R. Katsenbaum, (Ed.), *New Thoughts on Old Age* (pp. 41-60). N. Y.: Springer Publishing Company, Inc.

Miller, W. R., and Brown, S. A. (1997). "Why Psychologists

. . . .

Should Treat Alcohol and Drug Problems." *American Psychologist*, *52*, pp. 1269-79.

Newman, B. K., Reinecke, D. R. and Kurtz, A. L. (Fall 1996). "Why Be Moral: Humanist and Behavioral Perspectives." *The Behavior Analyst*, 19 (2), pp. 273-80.

Pierce, J. (January 14, 1998). An interview aired over Public Radio, *Insight and Outlook*.

Rae, S. (1991, June/July). "Wrapping the Human Package." *Modern Maturity*, 134 (3), pp. 72-94.

Reed, C. (1994, February). *A Parent's Approach to Solving Some Behavior Problems*. Found in G. Latham's *What's a Parent to Do?* (1997). Salt Lake City: Deseret Book.

Resnick, M. D., Bearman, P. S., Blum, R. W., Bauman, K. E., Harris, K. M., Jones, J., Tabor, J., Beuhring, T., Sieving, T. R., Shew, M., Ireland, M., Bearinger, L. H., and Udry, J. R. (September 10, 1997). "Protecting Adolescents from Harm: Findings from the National Longitudonial Study of Adolescent Health. JAMA, 278 (10), 823-32.

Roderick, J. (1994, January 9). An Inept Ruler and the 20th Century's Greatest Revolutionary. *The Logan Herald Journal*, pp. 17-18.

Sidman, M. (1989). *Coercion and Its Fallout*. Boston, Mass.: Authors Cooperative, Inc.

Staff (1989, December, Vol 1X, No. 12). "Hugging." *Hope Healthletter*, p. 6.

Sulzer-Azaroff, B., and Mayer, G. R. (1991). *Behavior Analysis for Lasting Change*. San Francisco: Holt, Rinehart, and Winston, Inc.

. . . .

Taylor, I. and O'Reilly, M. (Spring, 1997). "Toward a Functional Analysis of Private Verbal Self Regulations. *Journal of Applied Behavior Analysis*, 30 (1), pp. 43-58.

Walker, H., Colvin, G., and Ramsey, E. (1995). *Anti-Social Behavior in School: Strategies and Best Practices*. Pacific Grove, Calif.: Brooks/Cole Publishing Co., pp. 24–29.

Wyatt, W. J. (Ed.) (Summer, 1997). Infants' Brains Wait for Experiences to Shape Rational Thinking. *Behavior Analysis Digest*, 9 (2).

Suggested Readings

Antisocial Behavior in School: Strategies and Best Practices (1995), by Hill Walker, Geoff Colvin, and Elizabeth Ramsey. Pacific Grove, Calif.: Brooks/Cole Publishing Co.

How to Keep Your Kids from Driving You Crazy (1997), by P. S. Bender. N.Y.: John Wiley and Sons.

Coercion and Its Fallout (1989), by Murray Sidman. Boston Mass.: Authors Cooperative.

How to Talk So Kids Will Listen & Listen So Kids Will Talk (1980), by A. Faber, & E. Mazlish. N. Y.: Avon Books.

Families (1975) by Gerald Patterson. Champaign, Ill.: Research Press.

First Course in Applied Behavior Analysis (1998), by Paul Chance. Pacific Grove, Calif.: Brooks/Cole Publishing Co.

The Power of Positive Parenting: A Wonderful Way to Raise Children (1994), by Glenn I. Latham. Logan, Utah: P & T ink.

Living with Children (1976), by Gerald Patterson. Champaign, Ill.: Research Press.

. . . .

Teenagers and Parents: 10 Steps for a Better Relationship (1996) by Roger McIntire. Columbia, Md.: Summit Crossroads Press.

Meaningful Differences in the Everyday Experience of Young American Children (1995), by Betty Hart and Todd R. Risley. Baltimore, Md.: Paul H. Brooks Publishing Co.

Parents and Adolescents: Living Together (Part 1: The basics, 1987; and Part 2: Family problem solving, 1989;) by Gerald Patterson and Marion Forgatch. Eugene, Oreg.: Castalia Publishing Co.

S.O.S. Help for Parents: A Practical Guide for Handling Common Everyday Behavior Problems (1985), by Lynn Clark. Parents Press.

The Good Kid Book (1979), by Howard N. Sloane. Champaign, Ill.: Research Press.

The Parenting Challenge: Your Child's Behavior from 6 to 12 (1991), by Arnold Reincover. N.Y.: Pocket Books.

What's a Parent to Do? Solving Family Problems in a Christlike Way (1997), by Glenn I. Latham. Salt Lake City: Deseret Book Co.

Index

. . . .

Index

About the Author

Glenn I. Latham received his bachelor's and master's degrees from the University of Utah and his doctorate in education from Utah State University, where he is a professor emeritus of education. He has been a public school teacher and a school administrator, and is a nationally and internationally recognized scholar of the behavioral sciences.

Dr. Latham lectured extensively on the management of human behavior in home and school settings, and has authored seven books and numerous journal articles and technical papers on how to create "safe" home and classroom environments.

He and his wife, Louise, are the parents of six children and a growing treasury of grandchildren and great-grandchildren.